Networking Is a Curable Condition

Or

How I became an accidental marketer and ended up writing this
book that you just bought

Are you struggling to find a job?
Are you struggling to make sales?
Are you struggling to find ways to help your employees
differentiate themselves from everyone else?

If so, this book is for you.

Stand Out
Be Memorable
Differentiate Yourself
Tout Your Skills
Make Connections
Achieve Your Goals
Advance to the Next Door

Legal Mumbo Jumbo

Networking Is a Curable Condition
Version 1.

ISBN: 978-1512062632

The author reserves the right to make revisions and changes to this work. Doing such a thing will result in a Version 2. If the author pulls that stunt again, Version 3 might result. This might be repeated *ad infinitum*. So feel fortunate you are only reading this thing and not writing it.

Table of Contents

The People Responsible for What You Are about to Read

Author: Bill Snow

Bill Snow is an investment banker, M&A expert, writer, speaker, optimist, loud mouth, idea guy, deal guy, hack golfer, negotiator, music lover, and deal closer. He is the author of *Mergers & Acquisitions For Dummies* (Wiley) and *Venture Capital 101* (an e-book before we had e-books). The "For Dummies" book was the direct result of Bill's first foray into accidental marketing. Please, go buy a copy. He'll make 75 cents.

You can contact Bill at bill@billsnow.com. Visit him on the web at www.billsnow.com.

Facebook: https://www.facebook.com/BillSnowFanPage
LinkedIn: http://www.linkedin.com/in/billsnow
Twitter: http://www.twitter.com/bill_snow

Cover Illustrator: Larry Kaminsky

Larry Kaminsky is an innovative and multi-dimensional graphic designer, illustrator, and art director. He has strong conceptual and visual abilities, coupled with a comprehensive understanding of big picture strategic marketing and branding. Throughout his career, Larry has produced work for highly recognized brands including Coca-Cola, Kellogg's, Tyson, Wrigley, Subway, Yahoo!, OfficeMax, PayPal, Whirlpool, Siemens, Tampico Beverages, CDW, with industry experience across CPG, QSR, Financial, Sports/Entertainment, B2B/B2C, Food/Beverage, CPG, E-commerce, Publishing and many others.

You can contact Larry at larkaminsky@gmail.com. Visit him on the web at www.pixelballdesign.com.

LinkedIn: http://www.linkedin.com/in/larkaminsky
Twitter: https://twitter.com/larkaminsky

Editor and Proofreader: Amanda Brown

Amanda Brown is a detail-oriented copy editor and proofreader, music lover, devout environmentalist, and an engineer in her spare time. Her copy editing and proofreading experience runs the gamut from nonfiction business, military, and natural living books to historical fiction, science fiction, mystery, and romance. She currently works with several publishing companies

including Black Irish Books and Summerhouse Publishing as well as a plethora of independent authors. She always welcomes new ideas, warped humor, and enthralling projects.

You can contact Amanda at amandabrownedits@gmail.com.

A note on the formatting

This is the paper version of *Networking Is A Curable Condition*. As a result, this book has some very minor formatting differences compared to its electronic cousins. And yes, some pages were left blank on purpose.

Dedication

To lifelong learners. To late bloomers. To those who have tried and failed and are trying to gin up the courage again. To those who haven't yet failed, trust me, your time is coming. But don't worry, you won't be remembered for how you failed...you'll be remember for how you tried again.

Author's Acknowledgments

First and foremost, I owe a debt of gratitude to Larry Gard of Hamilton-Chase Consulting. Larry was the ringleader who set up my initial presentation, called "How to Avoid Being Networked to Death," for the University Club of Chicago's networking group in May 2013. I also owe a debt of gratitude to Bruce Schoumacher of Querrey Harrow. Bruce set up the networking coffee with Larry that led to the speaking engagement.

I also owe a debt of gratitude to Peter Converse, also of Querrey Harrow. Peter was one of only two people to show up to my June 2012 networking event. We ended up having a great conversation over a couple of beers and I am very glad we connected. Ironically, this event was the subject of a rather snide write-up by the late Ron May:

"The May Report: 6/11/2012: It will take me too long to write a long headline, but I'm still rolling on the floor laughing at the list of no-timers, has beens, and old timers who will be at Bill Snow's gathering for drinks at Bar Louie in River North on Wednesday evening, but I'll be at the Catapult open house — maybe I can make it after the open house, but for now let's call the Bill Snow event the Who's Who of Who Cares, and it's such a contrast to Built in Chicago and the pi** and vinegar exhibited by the fresh blooded entrepreneurs at 1871."[1]

Let this be a lesson to everyone. Networking isn't about talking to as many people as possible; networking is about connecting with the right people. Without my attempt to bring together a small group of people for no other purpose other than to get to know each other, I never would have met Peter, and in turn I would have never met his partner Bruce, and in turn I would never have met Larry nor had the opportunity to put together a presentation that eventually turned into this book you're reading.

Funny how that works.

Ben Rowland is also owed a thank you. Ben is a former colleague (yet another successful alumnus from the failed Vcaptial) and he runs a web development company. Ben was the one who pointed out the folly of the website with four bios and no clear path with whom to connect. You'll read about that shortly.

Jim Huguelet is the consultant who sent me a dozen logo golf balls as a thank you after we had a meeting so he could pick my brain about the M&A process. The golf ball pitch idea was developed as a confluence of Jim's generosity and my wildly errant drives. You'll read about that shortly.

Jay Leonard is the thirty-something ringleader of a group of professionals who get together in what I dubbed the "Hamburger Club." You'll read about that shortly.

As always, I need to thank the Internet because without you none of this would have been possible.

And lastly, to my fabulous friend: Muses are uncommon and rarely found, so thank you for being you. Who would have thunk? So many years. So far. So close.

---

[1] *http://themayreport.com/2012/06/11/the-may-report-6112012-it-will-take-me-too-long-to-write-a-long-headline-but-im-still-rolling-on-the-floor-laughing-at-the-list-of-no-timers-has-beens-and-old-timers-who-will-be-at-bill-snow/*

For Those about to Read...Cool Words from Cool People about Networking Is a Curable Condition

"I first met Bill through networking and found our meeting to be one of the most interesting and entertaining of my career. His ability to tell a story and keep things simple makes this book not only very readable, but also tremendously useful! It should be a must read for anyone who networks!"

~Brent Novoselsky, ChFC®
Vice President, Wealth Management, GCG Financial and former NFL tight end with the Chicago Bears and Minnesota Vikings.

"*Networking Is a Curable Condition* is entertaining to read and loaded with interesting examples of the many ways people sabotage their own efforts when it comes to meeting people. Better still, it offers a compelling perspective on the opportunities we all have to differentiate ourselves more meaningfully. Senior executives, team leaders, professionals looking to advance their careers, and job seekers will all benefit from Bill's wisdom."

~Rob Sullivan
Speaker, Executive Coach, and Author, Getting Your Foot in the Door When You Don't Have a Leg to Stand On (McGraw-Hill)

"Bill Snow's latest book, *Networking Is a Curable Condition*, is a smart, occasionally irreverent look at our hapless attempts to connect with others. He cuts through the platitudes and pabulum that pass for networking advice these days and focuses on the finer points of building business relationships. Bill wisely notes, "You'll never stand out if you strive to be the best at fitting in." And yet he makes it clear that you should be memorable not because of brashness, but because of how you treat others. Bill's networking strategy calls for good cheer, generosity, and a touch of humility. Here too he strikes the right balance; he is self-effacing without being self-erasing. Even the most seasoned networker will find some thought-provoking points in this book, and those new to networking should read it twice."

~Larry Gard, President, Hamilton-Chase Consulting

"Entertaining and informative, *Networking Is a Curable Condition* nails the message that successful networking about giving, not asking. Bill kept me chuckling as he humbly shares his journey to networking success. I wish I'd read this earlier in my career!"

~Cathy Carroll, President, Legacy Onward: Executive Coaching services for family businesses

"Bill has a wealth of knowledge and is a subject matter expert in the Merger and Acquisition field. His presentations and writings are clear, informative, and entertaining as well."

~Steve Callisher, Vice President, The Mentor Group

"*Networking Is a Curable Condition* is a must read for anyone looking for a better way to expand business opportunities. The unique aspect of the book is that it goes through real life examples and provides advice that can be applied to everyday business. I wish this book were written thirty-two years ago when I started my career."

~James Snyder, Partner, Ice Miller LLP

"Bill Snow has written a valuable book containing helpful tips for both those persons who consider themselves experts in networking and those who are just realizing that great opportunities await them if they only can meet the right people. A must for everyone."

~Bruce Schoumacher, Partner, Querrey Harrow

"Bill Snow has every right to share his approach to networking. Honestly, I thought I took a thoughtful, well-organized and creative approach to networking...and then I read Bill's book. A true master of his craft. Honest and good hearted, Bill brings it all."

~Jay Leonard, Principal, Bernstein Private Wealth Management

"Bill Snow's latest effort explodes the myths that too many professionals have about networking. His "tell it like it is" style will help you focus your most precious resource — time — on developing meaningful relationships where you can both give and receive true value. If you're looking for the antidote to a case of "networking indigestion," you'll find it in *Networking Is a Curable Condition*.

~Jim Huguelet, President, The Huguelet Group LLC

Networked to Death

[net-wurkt to deth] or [en-tee-dee]

Idiom

1. the act of hanging around with your peers, competitors, and friends and expecting them to buy something from you

2. extreme career weariness resulting from the failure to sell your product or service despite your endless participation in events with your peers, competitors, and friends

3. reality TV show idea where we lock an insurance sales person and an IT sales person in a room and neither is permitted to leave until one sells something to the other one

Introduction

This book developed following a series of speeches I gave on the topic of networking and marketing and differentiation and self-publishing. In early spring 2013, I was at the University Club of Chicago having coffee with some professionals. As I relayed some humorous asides, anecdotes, and the occasional insight about how I ended up being contacted by a publisher to write a book, one of my coffee-mates remarked that I should give a presentation to their networking group. Being the ham I am, I naturally accepted the offer.

I called the presentation "(How to Avoid Being) Networked to Death." I subtitled it, "or how I became an accidental marketer and ended up talking to you today." The concept of being "networked to death" started as a Facebook joke I shared with my friends. I said I had a TV show idea where we lock an insurance sales person and an IT sales person in a room and neither is permitted to leave until one sells something to the other. We'll call the show, "Networked to Death."

A mild chuckle resulted from that post and then the comment was forgotten. A few months later, I was scrolling through my Facebook posts and I rediscovered the post. As I thought about the joke, I realized it really wasn't a joke...being networked to death is the unfortunate outcome for far too many professionals.

In fact, I was guilty of being networked to death. I spent far too much time with my friends, competitors, and peers.

The opposite of being networked to death is doing things that open doors. The "life is a series of doors" speech is a lesson I heard from my father countless times. I think he began giving me the "life is a series of doors" lesson when I was about four.

According to the lesson, life is a series of doors. You can't open any of those doors; someone on the other side has to open that door for you. All you can do is present yourself in the best light possible and hope that someone opens a door. Once you pass through a door, you move forward until you face another door, and the process is repeated.

As I looked back on my career and examined what worked and what didn't work, I realized a simple truth — doors opened for me when I had something to offer. I also realized that doing my best to fit in and act like everyone else was a technique that never paid dividends. As I've said many times — you'll never stand out if you strive to be the best at fitting in."

What You Will Find in This Book

The story you are about to read is based on that presentation. I hope some of my experiences and insights will be a boon to you as you try to break into a profession, develop a career, further your career, sell a product or service, or encourage your employees to connect, stand out, and further their development as professionals and humans. Seriously.

What You Will <u>Not</u> Find in This Book

What this book is _not_ about is providing you with all the answers. I purposefully avoid providing shortcuts and check lists. Those are tactics. I do not want people to necessarily copy my tactics. Instead, the reader is encouraged to focus on the strategies of differentiating and standing out. As I have said many times — you have to figure out some things on your own.

That said, at the end of each part I have a "Reader Homework" section where I ask you to ask yourself questions. Hopefully this will help you build your own framework for success. You don't have to do what I did. Do what works for you.

The Goals for This Book:
- Find your talent
- Shore up your weaknesses
- Get doors to open by offering something
- Communicate effectively
- Be memorable
- Get results

This book deals with how professionals of all stripes and sizes can stand out in a world that is asking. All that asking becomes background noise, and if you continue to do the same things in the same ways as everyone else, you will probably end up with the same result as everyone else. I call this the eardrum buzzsaw of white noise. This book is about how you can avoid that eardrum buzzsaw.

And avoiding the eardrum buzzsaw starts with finding your talent.

Chapter 1

A Personal Brand Cures Bad Networking

- Your personal brand is your talent
- Success is difficult to obtain unless you have a grasp of your talents
- Take the time to figure out what you do better/differently than others
- Develop that talent; don't rest on your laurels
- Don't wait for the world to bestow a title on you. Proclaim yourself the expert in something...but do your homework and be prepared.

Venture Capital 101

In 2000, coming on the heels of working for a failed angel funded startup, I pestered and cajoled a venture funded startup until they relented and gave me a job. The startup was an exchange between entrepreneurs and venture capital firms and was supposed to efficiently link startups with the right venture capital investor. Interesting concept, but it didn't work for a multitude of reasons.

The positive takeaway from that experience was, for the first time in my so-called career, I learned what venture capitalists (VCs) wanted to see. More presciently for my caustic and devious writing style, I learned what caused VCs to run for the hills.

Not surprisingly, prior to getting involved in the venture capital world, I was doing everything wrong.

The venture capital funded startup eventually went the way of the dodo and by the spring of 2003, I found myself in the midst of further career indifference. By good fortune, I had connected with the CEO of another startup and we engaged in serious discussions about raising capital. The CEO was of a mind to retain my services for this capital raise. "Career indifference, be damned!" I thought. Here was a real opportunity staring me in the face. And better still, the CEO was on board with retaining (and paying for) my services.

The door was ajar.

Part of my business development process was to pay homage to the chairman of the startup. The chairman was the individual who had provided all of the company's funding to date — a couple million dollars. This was a meeting that I did not take lightly, but I was highly confident that I would connect with the chairman and my career as a high profile capital finder for world changing startups was about to commence.

Instead, the chairman and I clashed on the process of raising funds, and probably most damning of all, valuation expectations. I pointedly told the chairman I thought his valuation expectations were probably out of line with what a VC would value the company.

The chairman pointedly retorted by asking me, "What the #$%@ do you know about venture capital?"

The door slammed shut.

More than merely being disappointed with the outcome of the meeting, I found myself angry and frustrated. Angry with the chairman, who despite his success and affluence, really didn't know much about venture capital, and frustrated with myself for not being able to adequately articulate the many, many errors the chairman was making about venture capital.

Prior to the "what the bleep do you know" meeting, and in fact, prior to the demise of my venture-backed employer, I had been working on an article that described the many fallacies early stage entrepreneurs have about venture capital. In the wake of the disastrous meeting, I began working anew on that venture capital article.

Well, I didn't merely work. I was incensed about the "what the bleep do you know" meeting and I took out my frustrations and anger on my poor keyboard. As I added more and more ideas and observations, I realized the article was getting long. So I thought I would break it up into a two-part article. Then I thought it would be a three-part article. Then a four-part article. Maybe a ten-part article.

Then I thought, *Why not make it into a book?* I wove a narrative into the mistakes and misconceptions that many entrepreneurs have about venture capital. That narrative was loaded with pop culture references and, in fact, the development of the fictional company using the names of the Rolling Stones (Mick, Keith, Brian, Charlie, and Bill) for the entrepreneurs who invented and marketed a product to help keep dogs, black labs in particular, from making messes.

The book also made references to the Rat Pack, Led Zeppelin, Alice Cooper, Husker Du, and Iggy Pop. I memorialized my dog, Iggy, by naming the fictional venture capital company after him, and of course, the fictional product was based on my real-life experiences of living with a loyal, lovable, and sweet but ultimately shed-prone black lab. And since I was now having fun with the book, I cheekily claimed the book used Keith Richards' guitar tuning from Brown Sugar as a paradigm for venture capital.

But more than merely having some fun, the book took the reader on a funding journey from idea to venture capital to exit and all points in between. The working title of the original article was "Venture Capital 101" and absent anything better, I used that name for the final product.

Once I was done with my little treatise on venture capital, my next thought was, *Well, tough guy, big deal...what do you do with it?*

The Accidental Offerer

During the same time I was writing *Venture Capital 101*, I was out of work. So I did what most unemployed people do when they have nothing to do — I hit the networking scene. Like most other unemployed people, I liked to use euphemisms such as "I'm between opportunities" to explain my lack of current vocation. And since I was from a failed dot-com, I liked to say I was "between servers."

I had no idea what to do at these networking events. I met a lot of great people, and I am still in contact with many of them, but I quickly discerned that everyone was essentially doing a variation of the same thing — asking. Everyone was asking for something — for money and jobs and advice and help.

Lest you think these events where a total waste of time, they were not — Beer was involved.

Sales people, nominally selling products and services that no one at these events needed (nor often had the means to afford), also populated these events. These sales people spent inordinate amounts of time hanging out with their fellow networkers asking them to buy things while fending off other askers who were busy asking for an introduction to someone who might buy something or give them a job.

This was madness!

I've never been much of a joiner, so I quickly rejected the "ask" approach that everyone else was using. I did not want to be yet another in a long line of people asking for something the other party was unable (or unwilling) to provide. I decided instead of asking, I would follow up meetings by sending an email that basically said, "Nice to meet you...here's that book I talked about." I attached a PDF of *Venture Capital 101* and eventually, I put it up for download on my website.

I did not realize at the time, but I was offering something to the other party — a book, loaded with humor and insights. And better yet, the price was right. Those early editions of *Venture Capital 101* carried the price point of "Free! And worth the price."

I found my talent, my skill. I found what I could offer others and by extension, I created a personal brand for myself. I was the guy who knew all about venture capital and could explain it in very simple, easy to understand style. I was a capable writer.

My Talent: Writing

About a decade prior to writing *Venture Capital 101*, I began writing some silly, inane little newsletters for the intent of documenting (and, uh, embellishing) the crazy twenty-something years of my circle of friends. The first newsletter was a spur of the moment affair. I had a couple of thoughts in my head and I simply wrote them down, put them in a newsletter format, and mailed a few dozen copies.

The newsletter was a hit. People enjoyed reading about themselves and I found I enjoyed writing, creating and inventing personas and situations, and of course, teasing my friends. Instead of merely a one-off exercise, I quickly decided I would challenge myself by writing a regular newsletter. My goals were simple: 1) mercilessly abuse my friends 2) improve my creative abilities 3) hone my technical writing skills.

In fact, shortly after sending out the first, spur of the moment newsletter, I decided I wanted to get to the point where I could sit in front of my computer, with no thoughts in my mind and nothing on the screen, and just create and invent. I wanted to train myself to be creative. This creative ability is something that decades later, continues to pay dividends for me. I worked my craft. I put my time in and practiced and got better.

I was a middling student in school, and except for some savant-like ability to ace math class without studying, I was a C student. My understanding of math came without trying; I just "got it" and more often than not, I could figure out where the lesson plan was headed even before the teacher covered a particular subject or made a certain point.

Based on my ability to set the curve in math with a total lack of effort, I applied the exact same "hands off" manner to my other classes, and — surprise, surprise! — I struggled. I remember English classes, in particular, as being frustrating for me. I just didn't "get it" when teachers talked about grammar and usage and motifs and structure. Parse a sentence? Moi? No way.

I eventually applied myself and through a lot of hard work of self discipline, I raised my other grades to Bs. But as I look back on those years, I may have achieved some level of decent proficiency in most classes, but I did not fully comprehended the lessons. My better grades were more the result of rote memorization than thorough understanding.

I bring this up because as I started writing those silly, inane newsletters I discovered I was a rather creative person. And the more I wrote the more I understood about grammar and usage and motifs and structure. I guess I was a late bloomer, but by the same token, I worked very hard to improve my skills.

Becoming a good writer is akin to training a dog. I had a dog for years; he was a good, loyal, gentle beast. People, especially those with hyper, manic, out-of-control dogs, would comment that my dog's behavior was basically luck of the draw. They viewed their dog's bad behavior as merely their dog's personality and not as a reflection of their poor leadership skills.

Numerous people told me my dog obviously "came out of the box" with a gentle temperament and a willingness to obey. They thought he was born with a natural predisposition to come when called, to walk at my pace on my left side in "heel" position, and to fetch a ball and drop it at my feet. The truth of the matter is I worked hard to train him by applying consistent and unyielding discipline.

Much like a well trained dog, I did not "come out of the box" with my skills. I had to work very hard to improve my shortcomings and to foster my creativity.

And I have no doubt that you, gentle reader, can do the same. Creativity can be fostered, but like any other skill, you have to work at it.

The Takeaway

The Condition: Lack of renown, lack of recognition, lack of knowing what you are good at.

The Cure: Development of a personal brand.

I didn't wait for the world to tell me I was knowledgeable about venture capital; I took the initiative and proclaimed myself an expert. I practiced the art of writing for years by following my love of creating and writing and making light of my friends. In fact, the goal I set for myself when I began writing my newsletters was to be able to sit in front of a computer with no thoughts in my head and nothing on the screen...and instantly begin to create. That is a skill that has served me very well over the years. And I did it merely because I enjoyed doing it.

The Result: People want to meet with a person, not the company behind the person.
This is a bitter pill to swallow for people who work for large, well-known companies. A personal brand can carry you farther than a strong brand name company on your business card.

Reader Homework: I encourage you to build your own framework. Don't copy me. Do your own thing! Here are the questions you should ask yourself at this point:
- What am I good at?
- Do I have skills? What are they?
- What do I enjoy doing?
- Do I have a personal brand?

Chapter 2

Offering Instead of Asking Cures Bad Networking

- Do something! No one cares about your talent unless you use it
- By doing something, especially something you love and enjoy, you develop and hone your talent
- If you have something you can offer others, they will respond in kind
- Be prepared to field offers
- Jump at every opportunity you get to demonstrate your skills

Venture Capital 101 Post Mortem

As *Venture Capital 101* made the Internet rounds, person after person forwarded it to another person, who in turn, forwarded to more people. And a curious thing happened. People thanked me! Total strangers, people from far off foreign and strange lands — Israel, South Africa, Russia, Japan, Ivory Coast, and even Schaumburg, Illinois — sent me emails thanking me for my little book.

Even more exciting, the holiest of the holies, venture capital firms, contacted me to thank me for writing what they all wanted to write. For the first time in my career, I received correspondence from a VC firm that did not include "for your protection and ours, we have professionally destroyed your business plan."

This newfound positive correspondence with venture capital firms had a downside. *Venture Capital 101* was essentially a "what not to do" book. The VC firms could now tell the great unwashed to "bugger off" by sending them to my book. Someone else would be the bad guy, the bearer of bad news, the source that told them, "You don't have a chance in hell."

I was also contacted by all manner of entrepreneurs, dangling job offers and partnerships and, naturally, investment opportunities. Some of the offers were crazy things. The offers that were not crazy things were slightly less than crazy things. For someone who was still trying to figure out his next move, having people call me up and offer me opportunities — no matter how crazy — was gratifying.

On a more positive front, a periodical contacted me and asked me to write a column. ePrairie was a product of the times, a technology and startup focused online periodical, replete with the *de rigueur*, small first letter and capitalized second letter. I wrote a column called, "VC101" and my style was called "a refreshing vacation from normalcy" and "candid, abrasive, and refreshingly hip!"

Eventually, enough people said I should sell it so I set up a website with a partner and we sold *Venture Capital 101* along with other products and services aimed at early stage entrepreneurs. Today, the book is for sale on Amazon via Kindle Digital Press.

Dog Catches Car

During this time, I remember thinking I was on to something, but I didn't know what. I remember having the feeling that I might be able to hit the accelerator and ramp up something, I just didn't know what.

Venture Capital 101 was an e-book before we had e-books. Kindle Digital Press, Lulu, and other self-publishing sites did not exist. And regrettably, I did not have an effective way to stay in touch with all the multitudes of people who contacted me: *Venture Capital 101* was prior to LinkedIn, Facebook, Twitter, and other social media.

The bottom line is I didn't know what to do with my modest bit of renown and success.

The Big Time Publisher Comes A-Knocking

Eventually I took a position with a boutique investment banking firm and began working on larger transactions. I handled deal execution, meaning I was the person who got on the phone and talked with potential buyers, sent them the materials, organized and led management meetings, and negotiated and closed deals. I loved it.

Venture Capital 101 was very much on the back burner of my career when Wiley Publishing, Inc., a behemoth "don't call us, we'll call you" type of outfit, called me. *Venture Capital 101* found its way to Hoboken, New Jersey, and an acquisitions editor at Wiley reached out to me to write a "For Dummies" book.

I immediately jumped at the chance to write a book. Concurrent with negotiating the contract, we discussed the subject of the book. Wiley's idea was *LBOs For Dummies*. When I asked, "Who is the target market for that book?" They responded, "The people on Wall Street doing those huge, billion dollar deals!"

I said that did not make sense to me because, despite the page one nature of those deals, the market for mega deals is very small. Only a handful of mega deals happen in a given year and the people who do those deals, from the Wall Street investment bankers to the executives at multibillion companies, tend to be very sophisticated, very experienced dealmakers.

In other words, I wasn't going to be able to teach them anything. To the contrary, I would be able to learn much more from them.

As I mulled over the idea of writing a book, I started to brainstorm on a different subject. *What's an LBO*, I thought, *but a way to finance the acquisition of a company?* LBO, which stands for "leveraged buy out," means using leverage (debt) to do a deal. So then the idea hit me: *Mergers & Acquisitions For Dummies*!

Wiley asked me who would buy the book. I said middle-market business owners. Deals in the middle-market might be for much smaller dollar amounts, but the middle-market has many, many more transactions than the small handful of blockbuster, mega-deals.

Wiley carefully considered my suggestion before responding, "Naw, Bill, that doesn't make sense."

The discussions then ceased and I largely forgot about the book.

The Big Time Publisher Comes A-Knocking Redux

Two years after the initial conversations about writing a book, Wiley came back to me with a new idea. They made sure to tell me, repeatedly and very clearly, that the idea was all theirs. While I might be slightly exaggerating the following exchange, our conversation went something like this:

"What's the book title?"

"*Mergers & Acquisitions For Dummies*! Now remember, Bill, we thought of it, not you."

"Wonderful idea!" I exclaimed. "I wish I thought of it."

"Good, glad you like it. Remember, we thought if it, not you."

"Pure genius," I said. "But tell me, who's the target market?"

"Again, we thought of this, not you. We think the target market should be middle-market business owners."

"I love it, great idea!"

"Thanks, Bill. Remember, we thought of it, not you."

Extra Credit Reading: How to Write a "For Dummies" Book

Now that I had an agreement in principle to write the book, I needed to submit an outline. At this point I still did not have a signed contract with the publisher. All I had was an agreement with someone to develop the idea. The idea still need to be approved by some sort of executive committee at Wiley. I have no idea who these people were or if they were even people. In fact, throughout the entire process, I never met anyone from the publisher. Everything was done by phone and email.

I began imagining the committee was a group of wizards or trolls or space aliens who somehow had the magic power to divine the relevance of a book idea merely by reading an outline. Eventually, in my mind, the group morphed into a single person that I called Grand Poobah.

The challenge I had with the outline was I never used an outline when I wrote. Prior to word processing programs I wrote my school papers like countless others before me — longhand on a pad of paper...and then gave the document to my mother to type.

I always found this a frustrating method because I had a difficult time writing in a linear fashion. I was constantly refining the document and worse, my mind tended to jump from one section to another. I can remember using scissors to cut and paste paragraphs as I rearranged documents. I'm sure I'm not the only one who has done that.

When I went to college I lugged a typewriter with me. This meant my writing struggles intensified; now I had to do the actual typing. But during my college years, the computer became more prevalent. By my junior year, I discovered the computer lab and the greatest program I ever used — WordPerfect.

Granted, the only other program I used in those days was Lotus 1-2-3, but for a latent writer like me, WordPerfect was the typewriter of my dreams. At first, I used WordPerfect as a typewriter; I wrote longhand with pen and paper and then typed up the results on the computer. I could cut and paste with much more ease and the punitive punishment of having to retype an entire page after finding one, small typo, was eliminated. And of course, the spell-check feature, something we all take for granted today, was nothing short of miraculous.

I quickly realized I could dispense with the vestigial process of longhand and instead enter my thoughts directly into the computer. By doing this, I discovered I could finish my projects faster and with far better results. The computer was a perfect complement to my iterative, herky-jerky method of writing. I do not think I would be able to write anything without these modern tools, and I marvel at writers who wrote hundreds of pages of text by longhand and/or typewriter.

For me, my creativity and the writing medium converged and are one and the same. In fact, my creativity was fueled by being able to use a computer. So, having to come up with a detailed outline for the book was a process that caused much consternation. I was used to stream-of-consciousness writing and then iteratively editing and adjusting and moving and deleting and adding text until I had a final product.

Worse, Wiley was asking me for chapter page counts! When I asked how many pages of Microsoft Word translated to a page in a "For Dummies" book, I was told, "Dunno, page counts depend how the document is set up." When I told them I was using page size of 8.5 X 11 with 10 point Times New Roman fonts, single spaced with one inch margins, they told me, "Dunno, page counts depends on how many charts and graphs and images and bullet-point lists you have on a page."

While I had a rough idea in my mind of the flow of the book, I wanted to describe the basic steps in an M&A process. I figured that would be probably twenty or thirty pages, and from there I would iteratively add more information and anecdotes until I had three hundred plus pages. I didn't know what I was going to write or how the document would flow until I got my hands dirty and began to dig in and work.

So I struggled with writing an outline. I actually spent a fair amount of time pondering how many pages a certain chapter would have, "Hmmmm...should it be 27 pages, maybe 28 pages."

The first lesson of chapter page counts is they have to be even. Paper has two sides so therefore each chapter has to contain an even number of pages or else you'll have an empty page. And despite our best efforts, my book does have some empty pages!

The second lesson of page counts was to tell them anything they wanted to hear. "Bill, forty-eight pages is a bit long for a chapter; do you think you get that down to, say, twenty-six pages?"

"Oh, sure! No problem."

"And you have a short chapter here, only six pages, do you think you could make that a little longer, say fourteen pages?"

"Oh, sure! No problem."

Despite my acquiescence to the folly of determining page counts without knowing how many pages generated in Microsoft Word translated to how many pages in a "For Dummies" book, I continued to struggle to come up with a suitable outline. Attempt after attempt was rejected. I was failing at writing an outline in "Dummies Style," which as I thought about it, made me laugh.

After spending a couple of months of fruitlessly trying to write a suitable outline, my acquisitions editor asked me if he could take a swag at writing an outline. After rejecting countless outlines, he said he now had a pretty good idea of the subject and felt he would be able to rework my ideas in the rarified air of the much vaunted "Dummies Style."

Frankly, I was fed up at this point and figured the book would never happen in the "Dummies Style." I actually began plotting to write the book in my style ("Dumber than Dummies Style" I supposed) when my acquisitions editor emailed me his version of the outline.

After reading the outline, I was certain the project would never get off the ground. It was an unmitigated disaster. To get a sense of the outline's shortcomings, think of writing a cogent, well structured paragraph. Then think about randomly shuffling the words. All the words you wrote are still in the new paragraph, but those same words now lack context and meaning.

Now I was really fed up. I definitely thought the book deal would die an unceremonious death, "murdered by death" as that great poet Lemmy Kilmister might say, and this door, which was ajar, would slam shut. I told the acquisitions editor to go ahead and submit it.

Much to my surprise the Grand Poobah at Wiley green lighted the disaster.

Most people would be overjoyed at the prospects of writing a book. Ever the contrarian, my immediate thought was, "Oh, shoot, now I have to write it," and believe me, "shoot" is not the expletive I used. I had two problems: first, I had to write a book, and second, I had to write a book using an outline that made no sense.

I did the first thing anyone would do when faced with an overwhelming obstacle and an impossible task — I stalled for time. First, I was able to use the contract signing ritual to buy some time. This gave me a stay of execution of a few days. Fortunately, the contract had been negotiated two years earlier and as I later discovered, I got a pretty good advance for a first time author. Unfortunately, the contract had been negotiated two years earlier and therefore, the contract signing ritual only took a few days.

With the contract now fully executed, Wiley began pressuring me to write. So I initiated my second stall tactic. I pointed out the contract said I was due a payment upon signing the contract. Wiley told me to write. I said I needed to be paid first. "Write it," Wiley retorted. "Pay me," I replied. This went on for a couple of weeks.

After Wiley finally paid me, I threw out the Poobah-approved outline and wrote the book my way. After all the stalling and delays (roughly three months) I finally had a breakthrough and figured out what "Dummies Style" meant. "For Dummies" are resource books. While someone can read it cover to cover, the books are designed to be resources where people can use the index to look up specific topics for quick, discrete learning.

Armed with my newfound understanding of what I was being paid to do, I commenced to write. Wiley also supplied me with a Word template that I could use to set up my document to look exactly like a "For Dummies" book. This was a huge boon for me and I am grateful they were finally able to supply me with a very helpful visual tool.

I was able to lay out an entire document, and by finally being able to visualize that document, I was able to refine and adjust and change my intended flow of information. While not my preferred style to start a book with "page 1, chapter 1," I began to submit chapters.

Wiley was nervous when the submitted chapters did not correspond with the Poobah-approved outline. Well, to say they were nervous would be an understatement. They hit the wall. The advice I give to anyone else who is in the same situation is twofold: 1) have confidence in yourself and your abilities and 2) don't answer the phone or reply to emails.

I knew I had a good concept and frankly, since Wiley had since paid me for the work, I had the power in the situation.

I was fortunate to have a good editor and good proofreader and I continued to enhance and improve my skills. Probably the biggest lesson I got from writing the book was banishing expletive constructions from my writing. And as much as possible, from my speech, too.

The actual writing took just less than four months. The construction of the approved outline (which I immediately disregarded) took three months.

The only other "For Dummies" book I could write is *How to Write a 'For Dummies' Book For Dummies.*

The Accidental Marketer

I received my first copy of the book just before it was released. Like a kid at Christmas, I tore open the package. I remember being proud of myself. After all, writing a book is a goal for many people, a "bucket list" item if you will. I literally patted myself on the back.

This lasted about a second and a half as I thought, *Well, tough guy, big deal…what do you do with it?* I realized writing the book was only part of the process; marketing the other part. As I quickly figured out, marketing was left to the devices of the author and I realized I didn't have a clue about marketing. Ever the quick one, I suppose a clue was the PDF booklet Wiley sent me describing methods to market the book. Wiley called it the *Author Tool Kit For Dummies*. I referred to is as the *How to Market Your For Dummies Book For Dummies*.

I was so focused on plotting the flow of information, and of course, doing the actual writing, I did not think about how I would market it. Never crossed my mind. As I stood in my living room, with its empty walls, holding my book, I began thinking about my strengths and weakness. Writing was a strength; visual design was not. I thought I was pretty good at sales; I was clueless about marketing.

This "strengths and weakness" issue is something so core to all of us, yet far too many of us don't put much thought into it. I was certainly guilty. Writing my book caused me to give serious consideration to mine.

"What are your strengths and weaknesses?" is a lazy interview question. I think we all get asked this question when we are twenty-two and looking for our first post-college job. It is a bad question because it begets generic answers: "I work hard," or "I'm a people person," or "I'm good at solving problems," and so on.

The typical twenty-two-year-old mind figures the weakness part of the question is actually a trick and therefore decides to phrase the weakness in the form of a strength: "I work so hard I sometimes irate people."

A more honest and truly reflective answer for the typical twenty-two-year-old would be along the lines of, "My strength is drinking a lot of beer. My weakness is getting up in the morning, but that's in the past. I had a great time in college but I am here to work and move forward."

If you're a college kid and that isn't your answer…what is wrong with you?

If you are a recent or soon-to-be college grad, please don't think I am picking on you. I was into my forties before I could provide a reflective, insightful answer to the lazy interview question:

- My strength is writing; my weakness is design
- My strength is sales; my weakness is marketing

Million Dollar Advice:

If you are interviewing for a job and want to knock off someone's socks, prepare for the lazy interview question of "What are your strengths and weaknesses?" Provide an answer that is unique to you. In other words, avoid using generic descriptions that could apply to anyone. And be honest about your shortcomings. In fact, if you handle these questions adroitly, the position you are applying for should demand your skill set and not require your weaknesses. Ideally, other team members will be focused on those areas where you are weak.

The Takeaway

The Condition: Inability to get doors to open. Inability to find a career foothold. Inability to advance.

The Cure: Stop asking for interviews and opportunities. Instead, find your talents, fess up to your weakness, and focus on doing things that demonstrate your talents and interests and loves.

The Result: Had I set a goal of writing a book for a major publisher, that goal would not have been met. Instead, by following my bliss and doing things for me, doing things I enjoyed, and doing things that stretched and challenged my skills, I ended up being in a position of having something an outside entity wanted. Do what you enjoy, find your real talents, and pursue those talents merely for your own enjoyment...you'll be surprised at what develops as a result.

Reader Homework: I encourage you to build your own framework. Don't copy me. Do your own thing! Here are the questions you should ask yourself at this point:
- What are my strengths?
- What are my weaknesses?
- What am I doing to develop my skills and talents and interests?
- Am I taking chances or am I playing it too safe and turning down opportunities? When was the last time I took a "flier" on something?

Chapter 3

Self-Understanding Cures Bad Networking

- Networking is not having a list of people that you pester in some organized or unorganized manner; Networking is what you do to convey value to those people
- Understanding your strengths and weaknesses will help you figure out what value you can convey

Determine Strengths and Weaknesses

As I thought about my most basic strengths and weakness, I began to expand my list and tailor it toward my profession — middle-market investment banking. I started by brainstorming about all of the aspects of my work and the skills that are needed for each. Then I thought about what I liked to do and what I did not like to do. Then I designed a job description that would complement my skills and interests, and I identified the skills and interests my colleagues should have.

In this exercise, I set up a series of questions. I thought about aspects of my industry in an either/or approach. And while gray exists (I might like or enjoy aspects of each subject), I tried to determine which I liked or enjoyed *more*. I called this my Skill Set Segmentation and mine looked like this (my preferences/strengths/skills are **bolded** and **underlined**):

- **Written** vs. Visual
- **Phone** vs. Email
- Marketing vs. **Sales**
- **Meeting in person** vs. Phone conversation
- Student vs. **Educator**
- **Solver** vs. Learner
- **Advisor** vs. Listener
- **Creator/idea generator** vs. Implementer/plan executor
- **Offerer** vs. Asker
- **Negotiator** vs. Follow up
- Research vs. **Insights**
- Maintaining vs. **Creating**
- Compiling vs. **Analyzing**
- Design/format vs. **Content creation**
- **Telling** vs. Doing
- **Create original content** vs. Update and maintain
- Gather info vs. **Find connections & insights**
- **Conflict** vs. Consensus

The above list might help you as you try to figure out your skills/interests and by proxy, your weaknesses. But please note — this list was designed based on the intersection of my skills and my industry (middle-market investment banking). Instead of merely looking at my list, make a list based on the intersection of your skills/interests and your industry (or intended industry).

As I put this list together, I already had the benefit of knowing the skill silos of my industry. So for your benefit, let me give you a bit of the back-story. The work I do, middle-market investment banking, involves selling companies, buying companies, or raising capital for companies. To conduct that work, investment banking firms essentially divide the work into four silos:

- Origination, marketing, networking (winning the client, in other words)
- Materials preparation (compiling the sales documents, creating financial models, building a list of potential buyers/investors)
- Deal execution (calling buyers/investors, disseminating materials, soliciting offers, leading meetings, negotiating deals)
- The House (office expenses, compliance/broker-dealer requirements)

Exercise: Design Your Own Skill Set Segmentation

I suspect you may be interested in developing an Industry Skill Set list for your specific needs. So how can you do this? Every industry/profession is different, so I cannot offer you a one-size-fits-all approach. Instead, I can offer you some ideas about how you might be able to create your own Skill Set Segmentation.

Step 1. Design the skill silos for your industry. Think about the workflow in your industry from winning a client to doing the actual work, delivering the final product, and providing support services for employees doing that work. What are the steps? Who does what? How many different people are involved? What does each person do?

Step 2. Think about the main aspects of a business — sales/marketing, accounting/finance, management, operations — and think about what you like and dislike about each of these areas.

Step 3. If you are having trouble coming up with some questions, here are a few steps that might help spark your process:
- How are clients won? In other words, do you market to sales targets or do you get referrals?
- Do you like talking to other people or do you prefer doing analytical work?
- Are you better suited doing the nitty gritty work or do others do this better than you?
- Do you like creating and building? Or do you prefer documenting?
- Do you prefer talking to other people or do you prefer working alone.
- Are you comfortable in leadership roles or do you want someone to give you direction?
- Do you like nailing down process flows or are you better at coming up with rough ideas?

- Do you prefer working with fellow employees or with people outside the company?
- Do you like bookkeeping or would you prefer to write copy?

Step 4. Devise ten questions about your industry and your skill sets. If you come up with more than ten questions, that's perfectly ok!

Step 5. Pick your preferences.

Step 6. Now compare your preferences to what you currently do.

If you design your questions, you might be surprised at what you see. Are you currently doing what you love/enjoy/are good at, or are you doing things other than your strengths? If the former, you should be in a good place career-wise. If the latter, perhaps you need to make some changes.

Let's go back to my Industry Skill Sets and take a deeper look. Hopefully, you'll be able to see how they relate to my industry.

1. **Written** vs. Visual

I'm clearly far better at writing than I am with visual design. You only need to see the empty walls in my house or my PowerPoint presentation design "stylings" to confirm this! I can appreciate a well laid out document or a room with great design, but don't ask me to do that work. As a result, I don't worry about design anymore. Instead, I try to find people with a knack for it and then I defer to their expertise. I try to limit my input on design as much as possible.

2. **Phone** vs. Email

I love email. I use it all the time. But given my preference, especially if I have to communicate something sensitive, I prefer to talk with someone. Email is great to confirm a meeting or even as a tool to set up a time for a call, but email lacks inflection and context, and as a result, email can result in miscommunication and problems. Email is the communication tool of the passive-aggressive. It can be the path of least resistance, and I am guilty of falling into that trap, so I try to avoid email and I pick up the phone.

Keep your emails short, to the point, with a minimum of questions and to dos for the recipient. Otherwise, your email will blend in with the background noise of asks.

3. Marketing vs. **Sales**

As I previously wrote, I realized I was pretty good at sales but I did not know much (or anything) about marketing. Holding that first copy of *Mergers & Acquisitions For Dummies* is what got me thinking about the concept of marketing. Too many of us, myself included, tend to lump sales and marketing in to the same bucket. And while the two disciplines are closely related, they have a fundamental difference — Marketing is what you do in order to get a chance to make a sale.

4.   **Meeting in person** vs. Phone conversation
As with the phone vs. email dynamic in #2, the right method of communication depends upon what needs to be communicated. I much prefer the in person interaction of a meeting. This is especially important in my line work, M&A, because a meeting might involve multiple people — buyer, seller, buyer's advisor, seller's advisor — and an actual meeting is the most efficient way for all of those people to communicate.

5.   Student vs. **Educator**
For an indifferent student, someone who simply just didn't "get it" when I was in school, imagine my surprise when I discovered I was far better at explaining things to other people than I ever was having someone explain something to me. Occasionally in my life and career, I happened upon someone who was able to cut through the clutter and explain things very simply, very directly to me. In numerous written sources, I've referred to those people as "wise old sages." And in turn, I've tried to be that wise old sage for others.

6.   **Solver** vs. Learner
I have to get my hands dirty before I learn something. Often I was frustrated in school because, math duly exempted, I just didn't have the attention span or the right synapses to read and recall information with a high level of accuracy and insight. At best, I was a trained monkey, able to remember by rote some of the things I read but often without fully understanding the bigger picture.

I know now my preferred learning method is experiencing. But everyone has different preferences. More on this in a moment.

7.   **Advisor** vs. Listener
Except in rare occasions, I am not a good listener. And the older I get, the worse it gets. Is this a male thing — a function of millions of years of evolution? A result of societal influences? Who knows? Who cares!

The fact is I have figured out where my preference lies on this continuum. The challenge for me when I was in school and in my twenties, and for most young people, was I didn't know anything! Yeah, I could recite some facts and figures that I committed to memory, but my real insights didn't occur until I had a body of work to draw upon.

If you are young person, please keep this mind. Listen to those who have more experience than you, which, I hate to tell you, is just about everyone. But watch, listen, observe, and most of all, go experience. Advising is difficult when you have a limited amount of knowledge and insights. In all of your actions, in all of your decisions, try to take away something positive. Try to learn something about other people and yourself. Eventually, you'll have enough insights where you can be helpful to others.

8. **Creator/idea generator** vs. Implementer/plan executor
Yeah, sure, I can implement. I can execute someone's plan. But more often than not, I ended up creating my own path, doing things my way, explaining things to other people in a manner I thought made sense. When I managed retail managers, I wrote my own training manual (wish I still had a copy). When I got into the venture capital match making world, I ended up writing numerous articles, and eventually, a book, describing what works and what doesn't work.

And when I got into middle-market investment banking, I learned by doing, often designing my own plan, and eventually, I was able to memorialize those experiences in a book.

Other people are more comfortable with executing someone else's plan. Derisively, I've referred to this as "job in a box," but you know what? Some people are far better executing a plan than the creator of the plan. Neither is better or worse. Instead, I encourage you to figure out what you most comfortable doing.

9. **Offerer** vs. Asker
This was the initial insight I gained from writing *Mergers & Acquisitions For Dummies*. In fact, the "offerer vs asker" dichotomy is at the heart of this book and was the very genesis of changing the way I think and work.

The bottom line is — stop asking and focus on what you can do for the other person.

As I was writing this book, I was contacted by an executive who attended one of my presentations. He followed up with me with a list of private equity companies and commercial companies with which he was interested in connecting. But instead of asking me to forward his resume to people I know (a "Passive Ask" — more on that later) he studied the companies and came up with a thesis, something he could potentially offer these companies. This was a refreshing approach and the right way to connect with others.

I recommend that everyone, whether a job seeker or a sales person, think of what your target gets out of the bargain from dealing with you. If you focus solely on what you get, you are going to find the going is difficult.

10. **Negotiator** vs. Follow up

This dichotomy is very "Bill-career"-centric. My work as an investment banker requires a great deal of negotiating. And I enjoy it. I relish the verbal repartee, the mental jousting, the strategizing, the chess match, and ultimately, finding a solution that both sides find acceptable.

Where I quickly start to lose interest is when I have to follow up, month after month to get updated financials, for example. I need that information; I appreciate someone who can do that, but I prefer not to do it.

11. Research vs. **Insights**

Some people love doing research. I hate it. There. I said it. I wish I had the patience but I don't. I'm far better at working with results of someone's research, and based on my experiences, finding insights and connections. So I sought out a situation where other people do the research.

12. Maintaining vs. **Creating**

This is another Bill-centric career aspect. I enjoy the initial creation of materials, but I don't want to be the one responsible for constant updates and maintaining. I want to work with someone else who can handle this important part of our work.

13. Compiling vs. **Analyzing**

If you do a Google search for "Bill Snow financial model" you will see examples of my handiwork. One word of caution...don't pay for it! While I can compile and create spreadsheets until the cows come home, completing and repurposing data often comes at the expense of analyzing the data.

14. Design/format vs. **Content creation**

Another reason I prefer to avoid compiling data is because my design skills are, well, I don't have design skills. I'd rather focus on creating content and not worry about spending time making it look good. Other people have those skills.

15. **Telling** vs. Doing

As we advance in our careers, we find that we gain more leverage when we have others working under our direction. As you gain more knowledge and experience, you can often best utilize that knowledge and experience by directing other people to handle the details.

When you are starting out, you are probably going to be doing a lot of doing. Embrace it. Learn from others. Wait your time.

16. **Create original content** vs. Update and maintain
I would rather create the original contact and have others maintain it, update it, and keep it relevant and fresh. Frankly, other people have a much better eye than I do for the details necessary to keep content fresh and relevant. I'm much better at the creative aspect.

17. Gather info vs. **Find connections & insights**
When I am preoccupied with gathering information, I am not able to focus on analyzing that information. And as I mentioned above, I'm not thrilled by the prospects of doing research. But research is very important, and I need to utilize the results of research. So I much prefer working with people who are really able to sink their teeth into research.

18. **Conflict** vs. Consensus
When I've cited the "conflict vs. consensus" question in my presentation, people have often raised their hands and asked if I sought out conflict! The answer is, no, I don't seek conflict. Instead, I am comfortable dealing with the difficult parts of a negotiation. I've worked with investment bankers who want consensus; they want to get along with everyone. While noble, part of any negotiation is being able to hold your ground and press for your rights. You do not have to make the other side's case; that is their job.

Million Dollar Advice: Job Seekers, Stop Sending Resumes!
Simply sending out resumes is a low return way of finding an opportunity. Just as most of us know that cold calling offers a low return, so does cold mailing of resumes.

Instead, demonstrate that you understand some unique challenge faced by your intended industry and that you have a certain skill set to address that problem. The best way to do that is to get a full understanding of how your target industry silos its work and responsibilities. Earlier in this section I described the four buckets of my industry — origination, materials prep, execution, and the house. Each industry is different, of course, but take the time to figure out the specifics of your industry.

Next, divvy up your skills, interests, and weaknesses and think about them in context of your profession. As you do these tasks, you should be able to find some unique angle or interesting insight that will be of value to others. When you discover that angle or insight, you will find that you no longer have to passively ask someone else to do something with your resume. Instead, you will have something to offer. For extra credit, please review the marketing brief I created using this same method. The marketing brief is in Appendix A.

When you approach prospective employers, you can now do so from the perspective of understanding their needs and problems and how you can address those problems. If you employ this technique successfully, you'll find that your resume is the last thing you provide…not the first.

You can apply this same technique to your sales efforts. Instead of calling and asking, understand the other side's industry and challenges. Find something you can do to help someone else connect with sales targets. You'll find this strategy will open many more doors than merely asking for the business.

And Upon Further Reflection…
As I thought more about my strengths and weakness, I further refined my strength. As stated earlier, one of my strengths is my writing ability. But as I reflected further while giving presentation after presentation, I realized my key strength is an ability to explain complex things in a very simple, easy-to-understand style. I am a better teacher than student, or as I like to say, I'm much more discriminating than my teachers when picking students.

My weakness is no longer marketing; I've worked hard at improving that. I am still a disaster with visual design and now that I know that, I no longer worry about it. I actively strive to find others who have skills in that area. Also, I have difficulty starting and stopping. I procrastinate with my writing but when I get going, I have a difficult time stopping.

I also have a weakness for remembering people's names and faces! A bit odd for someone in the networking business. I handle that by owning up to that weakness and offering apologies and self-deprecating jokes. In other words, I do not attempt to mask or hide the weakness; I'm open and out in front with my weakness. I envy people with strong recall abilities. If you have that ability you should consider it a gift.

Learning How We Learn

Part of identifying your strengths and weaknesses is indentifying how you learn. If you are a supervisor in an organization, part of helping your people identify their strengths and weaknesses is identifying how they learn.

As I was preparing for my initial Networked to Death ("NTD") presentation, one of the organizers, Larry Gard, sent me an article about learning. Essentially, people learn in five general ways.

- Visual
- Auditory
- Reading
- Writing
- Kinesthetic

Visual learners prefer to observe and watch. Show these people a video! Let them observe others performing tasks. Auditory learners prefer to learn by listening. Books on tape are a great tool for them.

Reading preference learners can learn, if not master a subject, by reading a book. I didn't master accounting, heck, I didn't understand it until I needed to actually scour the company's books so I could understand where my money went!

Extra Credit Reading

I played a lot of basketball in college. I turned into a total gym rat. For years I played basketball at least five or six times a week. I loved it. I learned by throwing myself into games and slowly refining what I could do by experiencing the game. Once I had some level of proficiency, I was able to take instruction from others and hone my skills when others suggested improvements. Keeping my shooting arm perpendicular to the floor, for example.

A good friend of mine was the opposite. He was a reading-preference learner. He actually learned how to play the game by reading a book. This always amused me because when we played I could literally see the gears spinning in his head as he executed a move. He resembled Herman Munster and when his appearance was coupled with his rather robotic movements, I always chuckled at his playing style.

Not until years later, when I thought about learning preferences, did I realize this is what worked for him. We're all different, after all. One person's learning style may not be right for another person. The takeaway is to find what works for you (or your people).

Kinesthetic learners learn by doing. On some level I've known for years that I have to get my hands dirty and experience something before I can learn something. I don't think I'm unintelligent, but I was rarely a good test taker (except in math). I can master a subject; I just need to find a way to experience it instead of reading about it.

After I experience and learn, I have an ability to sit down and write about the subject. My writing is extremely iterative. I rarely work from A to Z. Instead, I write in a zigzag fashion, sometimes writing a sentence in one section before moving to another section where I might write a page. As I write, I often continue to learn. I gain further insights from the writing process. I wish someone had told me that when I was in school. In my opinion, traditional education favors the reading-preference learners.

The Takeaway

The Condition: Lack of understanding of your talents and skills.

The Cure: Find your strengths and tout them. Put yourself in positions to showcase those strengths. If need be, invent situations to show off those strengths. Don't wait for the world to acknowledge your strengths.

Embrace your weaknesses, fix what you can and for those things where you are hopeless...stop worrying about it! Tacitly acknowledge your weakness and find other people to shore up those weaknesses. Defer to their strengths and get out of their way.

The Result: I have a far better understanding of my skills and talents — and what I'm ***not*** good at — than I've ever had before. I know what I need to do to learn and find insights. And I know where I need other people with different talents and skills. I no longer concern myself with details where I don't have a skill. I defer to others. And I sleep much better at night!

Reader Homework: I encourage you to build your own framework. Don't copy me. Do your own thing! Here are the questions you should ask yourself at this point:
- Do I understand the basic flow of work in my industry? How are clients won? Who does what work? What are the deliverables? What is the timeline for this work?
- Have I segmented the skill sets in my industry into a series of questions? What do I like to do? What am I good at? What do I want to avoid? What am I bad at?

Chapter 4

The Game of Sales Cures Bad Networking

- Connecting with multitudes of people doesn't mean much if you're not generating sales.
- Understanding the difference between your sales targets and influencers will help you better utilize your time and efforts.
- Utilizing the right approach during networking meetings will increase your odds of developing fruitful professional relationships.
- Encouraging your people to develop personal brands can help them stand out from the crowd of people who look the same, act the same, and say the same things.

Why do we want to differentiate ourselves, our people, and our products/services from others? Why have I written this book? To make sales! Any insight or idea that you may have garnered from reading this book (and I hope you have had a least one "ah ha!" moment) is worthless unless you are able to generate leads and close deals.

So if the idea is to be able to take the lessons I've laid out and apply them so you and your people can better connect with people and get the type of result they seek, what are some techniques? To explain that, let's examine what I call the "Game of Sales."

Targets and Influencers...and the "Others"
The first rule of the Game of Sales is to determine who are your prospective clients ("Targets"). Who buys your product/service? If you are uncertain, here's a hint: whoever pays money for your product or service is your Target. If you don't know that by now, nothing in this book can help you. All of your professional networking should be predicated on getting a chance to be in front of your Targets. Remember, marketing is what we do to get a chance to make a sale.

The next rule is to determine who influences those Targets ("Influencers"). If you can go direct to your Targets, this step may be unnecessary. But for many of us, especially those selling a professional service, leads come from Influencers. If that applies to your industry or vocation, you want to identify the types of people who lead you to your Targets.

And the last rule is to determine who are the Others. Others are your friends, competitors, and peers. Unless a person actually makes the "buy" decision or leads you to a Target, that person is an Other.

I suppose going to a family reunion or a dinner party with old college friends or a backyard BBQ with the neighbors can accidently lead to a Target. Maybe your second cousin's new wife is in a profession that is in connection with your sales Targets and, just by happenstance, she had a conversation with a client who is in need of your product/service. Yes, this can happen from time to time, but I would view this as an outlier, not a viable sample.

Instead, go to the family reunion or party or BBQ with one goal in mind — have a good time. If business develops, great, but don't count on it.

Fuzzy or Concrete

Many sales professionals operate in the world of fuzzy sales and worse, most do not realize it. Fuzzy sales exist when the Target has no sense of urgency to make a buy decision. If you find yourself stuck in the endless cycles of "call me after the holidays, call me when the weather warms up, call me after the summer, call me after I take my kid to school, call me after the holidays" then you are in the world of fuzzy sales.

Your biggest competitor is not another firm offering something similar; your biggest competitor is the non-decision. Commercial bankers, wealth management professionals, investment bankers, and many, many other professionals operate in this world. You are not losing sales to *other firms*. You're losing sales because your prospects simply refrain from making a decision to hire *any firm*.

The mistake made by many sales professionals is to consider other firms to be their top competitors. When we find a Target, we like to think we are in "bake offs" where a decision will be made — and sometimes we are in those situations — but quite often our top competitors are no decision, radio silence, and stasis.

Think about your past prospects. How many of them hired other firms? How many just faded away? If the majority of your lost sales Targets hired another firm, you are clearly in the concrete sale world. If the majority of your lost sales Targets never made a decision, you are in the world of fuzzy sales.

Concrete Sales — Bake Off City, Baby!

When I use the term "concrete sales" I do not mean literally selling a coarse granular material embedded in cement. Instead, I refer to a Target that has a sense of urgency and will make a decision to hire a firm.

As an example, business valuation work is very much a concrete sale. Valuations are triggered by another event: a death, divorce, annual review, a partnership dispute, etc. Since multiple firms usually make a pitch to the prospect, I call this "bake off city." A decision will be made, but only one firm will win the valuation mandate.

If your sales efforts tend to be in the concrete world, you need to do what you can to differentiate yourself from your competitors, but more importantly, your goal should be to get as many at bats as possible. If you routinely win, say 20% of your pitches, you simply need more pitches.

Fuzzy Sales — Use Stasis Marketing

If you find yourself in the world of Fuzzy Sales, you want to employ tactics that battle silence and non-decision more than besting your competitors. You want to create a sense of urgency in your Targets. Tactics to create that urgency include:

- Offers, not Asks
- Valuable introductions
- Consistent touch points
- Messaging that runs counter to all the others
- Memorable persona

Tactic 1: Offers, not Asks.

For example, asking a prospect to meet to talk about their options is an "ask." Inviting the prospect to an event is an "offer." Reminding a referral source to "think of us when you have a client in need of our services" is an Ask. Actually, it is worse than an Ask, it is a "passive ask." Inquiring about their interest in participating in an event is an offer.

Passive Asks should be avoided because we are requesting another person to do our job. Instead of finding our own clients or our own job opportunities, we are asking someone else to do things we should do for ourselves. Most recipients of the Passive Ask will politely say, "Sure, I'll let you know when I find something that will be of interest," and then immediately forget about the conversation.

Offers tend to cut through the clutter of countless Asks and Passive Asks. That said, asking for the business is entirely appropriate and I am not suggesting we abandon the Ask. Instead, focusing on offers puts us in a much better position to eventually move to the Ask.

When I offer my prospects an invitation to an event, this offer allows me to communicate with prospects who may have gone radio silent. Instead of resorting to never-ending asks I am able to offer them an exclusive, special, and unique event.

Here's the rub in all of this offering. Prospects do not have to attend an event for me to receive a benefit. Simply inviting them tends to put me on a different level from other M&A advisors.

Extra Credit Reading: My Marketing

In my world (middle-market M&A), prospects are often referred to us from lawyers, accountants, wealth managers, and commercial bankers. I try to find something I can offer each of these groups of professionals.

For lawyers, accountants, and wealth managers I offer participation in business owner events. Not only does this put them in contact with business owners/executives, it allows them to market the event to their prospects, thus allowing them to offer something instead of asking for something.

Commercial banking is a commodity and differentiation is extremely difficult. Worse, getting M&A referrals from commercial bankers is difficult because when a business owner is selling the business, the new owner usually has a different banking relationship. This means the commercial banker will probably lose a client.

For commercial bankers I offer my networking presentation. Not only do I give this presentation gratis I also tell them I won't talk about my work (M&A) unless an attendee asks. Commercial bankers can stand out from the herd by inviting their prospects (and clients) to an event to hear some interesting, funny, and insightful observations about marketing, networking, and differentiation.

While I refrain from the "hard sell" during these presentations, I'm also assuming if I can get in front of enough business owners, eventually some will turn into prospects and clients. I also assume if I provide a service for commercial bankers, they'll think of me when they are in a position to make a referral.

Tactic 2: Valuable introductions
Take the time to understand the needs of your Target or Influencer and make introductions that actually help the person. Don't introduce competitors. Don't introduce lawyers to lawyers, don't introduce accountants to accountants, and so on. Obviously, the most valuable introduction is a possible client.

Making a valuable introduction demonstrates that you are thinking about the other person's business, and if you are able to make the right kinds of introductions, you will catapult to the top of that person's "gotta reciprocate or do business with" list.

When making an introduction, I try to make follow up as easy as possible. Instead of an introduction that includes the email addresses only and a nonspecific line that reads "You two should meet," I like to include each person's full contact information plus a couple of sentences explaining why I am making the introduction. My email introductions usually look something like this:

Subject line: Mutual introduction: Smith / Frankenson

Gentlemen,

Please accept this email as a mutual introduction. Frank is a lawyer with the firm of Smith, Smith, and Another Smith and he focuses on commercial transaction work, specifically M&A transactions. Franklin is the founder of Franklin's Bad Nickname, Inc., a company that gives people complicated nicknames. Franklin is considering a sale transaction for the company and might be in need of capable legal advice. I hope you two find this introduction helpful.

Frank Smith
Partner
Smith, Smith, and Another Smith
123 Main St
Suite 5200
Chicago, IL 60699
fsmith@notarealemailaddress.com
office: 312-555-5555
cell: 847-555-5555

Frank "Franklin" Frankenson
CEO/Founder
Franklin's Bad Nickname, Inc.
321 Commerce Ave
Suite 3A
Park Ridge, IL 60068
frank@gotabadnickname.com
Office: 847-555-5556
Cell: 312-555-5557

Good luck connecting!

Bill
[my full contact information is also included]

Tactic 3: Consistent touch points

In the land of Stasis, the last one who walks past the decision maker's door is the one who wins. A few years ago I was having coffee with a commercial banker. He was lamenting a recent loss — a Target he had been pursuing for years took his business to a competitor.

My banker friend was a bit miffed because he had been doing all the right things: lunches, golf, forwarding articles, etc. He got busy with other work and did not reach out to his Target for about six months. During that time, the Target had a need for a new commercial banking relationship and instead of calling my friend, the Target ended up using someone else...a competitor who just happened to cold call him at the right time.

In order to stay in the top of the minds of your prospects, put together a formula of when you are going to follow up with your prospects. If you use a customer relationship management (CRM) system, take full advantage of the ability to create groups. I have groups for my main professional connections (lawyers, accountants, wealth managers, commercial bankers), I have various prospect groups, I have a group for golfers, and so on. This system enables me to segregate my constituents and I can therefore market to different groups in different ways.

Tactic 4: Utilize messaging that runs counter to all the other askers
This is probably the easiest thing to say and most difficult to achieve. Whenever I can, I try to make my marketing emails memorable, different, daring, and funny. The best way I can explain this to show you some of my work. Please see Appendix B for some examples.

Your Targets and Influencers are busy and preoccupied. They are not grading you by how good you are at creating bland, prosaic, safe, and boring communications. If your messaging is the same as everyone else, how can you expect to break through the clutter of all those other asks? You can't. Your communication is merely wallpaper, boring and indistinguishable from the rest. And worse, it will get deleted before someone even reads it.

I cannot give you many examples of how to do this because I do not want my readers to merely ape things I have done to differentiate myself. Also, a one-size-fits-all approach will not work because readers of this book will come from myriads of industries and professions. What works for a lawyer might not work for someone in industrial sales, and what works for someone in industrial sales might not work for someone in retail. The key is for each of you to figure out what others in your industry are doing and saying...and then do something different.

Now that I have given my disclaimer, let me give you a couple of examples. As I was writing this book, I had a meeting with an acquaintance. She was in the midst of writing a book about family businesses and she mentioned she was trying to find a few more subjects to interview. I offered to send an email to some business owners I know, and frankly, owners I was *trying* to get to know. Business owners rightfully are weary of anyone making an overture because they feel they have a bull's-eye on their backs that reads, "SALES TARGET."

At my encouragement, my acquaintance drafted a one-page description of her book project and I emailed it to my network of about eight hundred business owners. I received over sixty replies, including over thirty very enthusiastic replies asking to be a part of the book. Of the people who declined, the emails were of the "thanks, but no" variety. No one asked me to stop sending emails.

I also received half a dozen replies from owners asking to speak to me about some aspect of their business, specifically as it relates to my line work. If I sent an email saying, "I want to sell your business for you," I doubt anyone would have replied and more likely than not, many of them would have asked me to never contact them again.

I want to provide value, I want to help, and I figure if I do that enough, and do it in a genuine manner, eventually enough people will raise their hands and say, "Bill, I'd like to talk to you about something."

Please remember, being daring and funny and different in your communication is not a license to be unprofessional or to do things that are untoward. If you would like some other examples of things I have done, please see appendices B and C of this book.

Tactic 5: Be memorable
Similar to utilizing messaging that runs counter to all others, do not be afraid of being memorable in person or on the phone. While the subject of differentiation can be the subject of unlimited books, I've found the following traits to being very useful in cultivating a memorable persona:
- Honesty
- Quick witted
- Funny
- Approachable
- Interesting insights
- Open minded
- Willingness to listen
- Confident body language
- Cool demeanor

In other words, strive to be you. Think about your friends. They are your friends because you are you, not because you put on airs or strive to be some sort of perfectly generic friend. You have a personality and that's why you have friends. Don't be afraid to use the same personality in your business exchanges.

Remember, you'll never stand out if you strive to be the best at fitting in. Your sales Targets and Influencers are not grading you by how well you look and act like everyone else. But they will remember you if you act and speak and communicate in memorable ways. And being memorable goes a long way toward winning business.

How to Handle Meetings

Part of the Game of Sales is having networking meetings with the people who might lead you to prospects. When I meet with people for the first time, I want to get to know the person. I do not ask for introductions to their clients and prospects. And while business occasionally occurs from an initial meeting, my goal is to merely get to know the other person and establish rapport. Talking about our respective businesses is important, of course, but often my main focus is talking about other subjects — sports, current events, family, favorite movies, books, and so on.

At initial meetings, I do not ask my new networking friend to introduce me to some unknown client (or prospect) before I even know if my new networking friend has someone for me to meet. Frankly, I find this approach to be a big turn off. If you ask for introductions before 1) gaining an understanding of the other person's business and 2) determining if they even have someone for you to meet, you will find more doors will slam shut than open.

If you are struggling to comprehend the above point, think of it another way. Let's say someone walks up to you and asks if you have any old bikes for sale. You tell the person you do not. The person continues to say, over and over, that he wants to buy used bikes and asks you to let him know when you have a used bike for sale or learn of anyone else selling used bikes. All attempts to have a conversation are scuttled because the person continues to ask, or dare I say pester you for something you do not have.

A version of this malady is when job seekers only talk about what they want: A job! On more than one occasion I have had meeting with a job seeker who has started the meeting by saying, "I hear you know a lot people...who can you introduce me to?"

Initial meetings that one sided — in other words, when one person wants the other person to provide something for free and without reciprocation — tend to end quickly and rarely result in second meetings. A good rule of thumb is if you are unwilling or unable to provide access to your clients or prospects, do not presume to immediately ask for entrée to the other person's clients and prospects.

Instead, you can help yourself by helping the other person connect with his prospects. Take the time to understand the other person's business and the challenges he faces. If you can help him open doors to his prospects, you have a much better chance of receiving something in exchange.

In networking meetings, I often describe how I want to focus on the unknown universe (prospects not yet on our collective radars) instead of trying to divvy up each other's known universe (clients and prospects). In other words, I am looking to work with other professionals in situations where we can pool our marketing resources to create new prospects for us both. Yes, I would welcome an introduction to the low hanging fruit of a current client or prospect (and I am always happy to make appropriate introductions to my clients and prospects), but I view those situations to be outliers.

Lastly, put down the phone! Focus on the person in front of you. If you constantly check emails and texts, you are essentially telling the person you are meeting that the most important person in the room is the person who has not yet called or emailed you.

How to Handle Networking Events
Here are five helpful tips to remember when hitting the networking scene.

1. Name tag on your right side
When attending networking events put your name tag on the right side. Many of us, probably because most of us are right handed, place name tags on our left side. Since we typically shake hands with our right hands, our right side turns toward the other person. These means our left side turns away.

If you place your name tag on your left side, the person shaking your hand will have a difficult time seeing you name. Putting your name tag on the right side will help people more easily see your name. For certain people who have trouble remembering names and faces (ahem...me!), the right side name tag is a huge help.

2. No passive asks
Passive asks are something we should always try to reduce and avoid, and nowhere is this more true than at networking events. Few things are more off-putting than meeting a pushy salesperson

for the first time. In other words, do not be this person! Develop rapport with people before you ask for business, and even then, tread lightly.

3. Look at people and speak up!
Networking events are often held in noisy, public places. When you speak with people, don't look at your shoes and talk under your breath. You need to make sure people can hear you. Speak up, make eye contact, and if necessary, learn to project your voice.

4. Shake hands like a grown up
Avoid the limp grasp. Instead, make sure you utilize a firm grip, but don't crush the other person's hand, either. Also, don't twist your hand, placing it on top of the other person's hand. This is an unconscious attempt at trying to take the dominant position. Lastly, do not look away when you shake hands, look the person in the eye.

5. Bring business cards
I am constantly surprised by how many times people show up at networking events without business cards. Always, upon pain of death, have a stack of business cards on your person. I always put my business card holder in my jacket pocket. On warm summer days, if I go to lunch sans jacket, I always put a couple of cards in my shirt pocket just in case I meet someone or run into someone with whom I have lost contact.

Yes, your business card contains your contact information, which is important for someone you just met, but the card can also act as a "forced" memory recall device for someone to follow up with you.

Extra Credit Reading: Rosebud Moment
{Spoiler alert!} If you have not seen *Citizen Kane* and do not want to know the ending of the moving, read no further!

In the great movie *Citizen Kane*, the word Rosebud is uttered by the protagonist, Charles Foster Kane, just before he dies. Rosebud becomes the mystery of the film. Who is Rosebud? Not until the end of the movie do we learn that Rosebud was a sled, a favorite childhood toy of Kane and memory of perhaps the last time he was truly happy.

How many times have you tried to win a client, only to be rebuked time and time again? How many reasons have you heard when you lost a prospect?

I've learned that quite often the reason you hear for not winning a client is different. Something else is at play. I call this the Rosebud moment.

A wealth manager once told me he had pursued a potential client, a business owner, for many years. Every time they met the prospect would agree that he needed to do estate planning but when push came to shove, the prospect would not hire the wealth manager. Nor anyone else.

Finally, after more than ten years of pursuit, the business owner told the wealth manager that he had a sister who owned a small piece of the company. The owner and his sister did not get along. In fact, they despised each other and had not spoken in years. This was the first time the wealth manager learned of the sister. The owner refrained from engaging in any sort of wealth planning because that would mean the sister would be involved.

Armed with this bit of information, the solution was easy: The wealth manager suggested that the owner buy out his sister's shares. When the deal was done, the sister was delighted to get a check and the business owner now owned 100% of the company. And most importantly — for the wealth manager — the owner finally was of a mind to hire someone to do the long procrastinated estate planning. The wealth manager in question finally won the business. The sister was Rosebud.

Quite often blockage to getting a sale is a Rosebud moment. The real reason is often not what we are told. The diligent sales professional will always keep this in mind and will constantly seek a new way to connect with a prospect. If you can figure out what is really at the heart of the decision (or lack thereof), you will have a much better chance of winning the business.

Encourage Your People to Develop Personal Brands

I am about as strong a booster you will find for the free enterprise system. By leaving people alone to pursue their own happiness, we foster a system that best breeds the actualization of abstract thought. We use our brains, not our backs, to earn our daily bread. We turn ideas in our heads into something tangible. This book is an example. I believe our creativity and problem solving is unlimited.

So I like companies. Big, small, medium sized, I like 'em all! I am not someone who bemoans corporate interests. People have the freedom to run their businesses as they see fit; people have the freedom to decide whether they want to patronize a particular business; people have the freedom to decide whether they want to be a part of a particular company's culture.

So, for the life of me, I cannot understand why far too many corporations, in particular large companies, do everything they can to tamp down the personalities of their employees. They limit their employees' use of social media, they prevent their employees from being interviewed by publications, and they even block attempts to write books.

A close personal friend of mine was once interviewed by the Wall Street Journal. When his employer, a Fortune 500 company, learned of the interview, the interview was quashed. The employer did not want anyone except the top executives of the company to appear in print, much less on the front page of the Wall Street Journal. My friend still bemoans the fact his woodcut image never saw the light of day. By the way, after hearing that story from my friend, I added to my bucket list…I want to get my woodcut image on the Wall Street Journal.

While writing this book another friend told me his employer prevented him from a publishing a book. This person is in sales and competes in a highly commoditized industry. People have a very difficult time standing out from their competitors. Everybody offers the same product and does so in the same way. Having something different to talk about can be the difference between gaining a client and coming in second place.

Whether those employers know it or not, they are telling their people to "look like everyone else, act like everyone else, speak like everyone else, do things like everyone else…but connect with people and win business!"

Managers and executives of large companies, you need to ask yourself, do you want automatons working to expand the greater glory of the mothership or do you want individuals working in concert with other individuals, connecting with others and winning business that they will bring back to the mothership?

Every time I've given my Networking presentation and asked that question, I always get some people who smile and nod in agreement to the first part of that question. At first, this surprised me. After all, I was talking about the greater glories of the personal brand. So I readily acknowledge that this is a difficult question. Companies spend huge amounts of money developing brands. People are hired to execute jobs for that brand and those people are paid for their efforts. That's a free exchange. Someone carving out a parallel path by creating a personal brand might not be working in the best interests of the brand that is paying them to generate business for the brand.

But then again, freeing your people to develop personal brands (that don't run afoul of the mothership's brand, of course) can be a powerful technique that will better enable those people to do what the brand wants — connect with people and make sales.

Granted, freeing your people to develop personal brands is a double edged sword. They can easily go to a greener pasture and take their business with them. Ultimately, this is a question for executives and managers, and while I would love to see more individuality in the corporate world, I understand your need to maintain and develop guardians of your brand. Just don't be too surprised when your best and brightest leave your ranks and your competitors win business at your expense.

The Takeaway

The Condition: Failure to connect with the right types of people.

The Cure: Determine the difference between Targets and Influencers and then figure out whether the sales process is a bake off between you and other providers or you are trying to make a sale with a Target that lacks urgency to make a decision. If your Target lacks a sense of urgency to make a decision, utilize messaging that is different from all others. Be different. Find something of value you can offer your Target.

The Result: This book is very much the result of my marketing and efforts to connect with people. While everything I do is a work in process and undoubtedly I'll update and adapt and change techniques and process as I move forward, what you are reading in this book is what I do to connect with people.

Reader Homework: I encourage you to build your own framework. Don't copy me. Do your own thing! Here are the questions you should ask yourself at this point:
- Are your sales fuzzy or concrete? If fuzzy, what are you doing to differentiate yourself? If concrete, what are you doing to get more at bats?
- What are you doing to develop a personal brand?
- Are you accepting of your employees developing a personal brand or do you want to restrain that? Do you run a risk of losing your best and brightest by restraining their personal brands?

Chapter 5

Knowledge about Sales Cures Bad Networking

- We all make mistakes. That's part of the condition of life.
- If you are smart, you can learn from the mistakes of others and if you're really smart, you can avoid committing those same mistakes. The world of networking is no different.

Networking Dos and Don'ts

One of the negatives about networking is seeing the many bad habits and mistaken assumptions people have about networking. Ironically, that's one of the best things about networking, too. Those errors are the counterbalance to the things that work, and without knowing what does not work, we would not know what does.

Without further ado, here is my list of networking Dos and Don'ts.

Do! Develop rapport

Networking does not count for anything if you do not develop rapport with people. Take the time to get to know someone. Don't push your product or service on them. Listen to the other person. Ask questions and get out of the way. Learn as much as possible about the other person and his needs and work concerns and problems and challenges. Be genuine. Be yourself.

Don't! Charge up the hill

Charging up the hill is what I call it when people constantly ask for the business. Yes, yes, in sales we need to ask for the business, but I believe the right things should be done at the right time. Coming on too strongly may push away a person who might later become a customer. If that person ultimately isn't a suitable Target, that person may become an Influencer that will lead you to a Target. Pushing too hard too fast too early simply means you run the risk of losing a longer-term relationship.

Do! Stay in front, stay top of mind;

Fair or not, in the game of sales the last person often wins. You can spend weeks or months or years pursuing a Target only to lose to a total stranger who just happens to sweep in at last moment — the exact moment when your Target is suddenly in need of your product/service — to win the business you have been pursuing.

While frustrating, that person was doing what you should have been doing...staying top of mind.

Don't! Be a taker

Years ago, back in my days of clueless networking, someone contacted me because he "wanted to network." This was shortly after I wrote *Venture Capital 101* and I was basking in the glow of not knowing what to do with my small bit of Internet fame and renown. When I asked this person what he meant, he explained very bluntly: "I want to know who you know."

I declined the meeting. While I suppose I should be grateful for his directness, his approach was totally off-putting. I was merely a vessel for his plan; he was offering nothing in exchange. I mention this story because too many of us unwittingly utilize the same approach when we "network" with others. Don't be a taker. Think of the other person first and foremost. If you can strive to find ways to help others, you will be surprised at how frequently doors will opened for you.

If you take away only one lesson from this book, this is it! Do not become known as a taker.

Do! Forgive others for their networking sins
Nobody is perfect. We all make mistakes. As frustrating as someone else's poor networking techniques may be, remember the following admonishment: But for the grace of clueless go I. Be willing to forgive and move on.

Don't! Use "Let's stay in touch" when responding to an email
Just like most people, I am guilty of this inane and meaningless phrase, but I am trying to wean myself from using it. If you really want to stay in touch with someone, set a meeting or a phone call. And if you really are planning to "stay in touch," set a reminder in your calendar and tell the person that you'll reach out again in a week or month or year.

Do! Have a reason or goal
Have a reason for reaching out to someone. Your overture might be for business reasons, personal friendship, asking a favor, offering something, but have a reason!

Extra Credit Reading
A few years ago, I was having a beer with a good friend. He was one of the first people I met when I went to college. After starting his career in public accounting in Chicago, he segued to wealth management and eventually relocated to Indianapolis.

As we had a beer, he engaged in behavior that is very odd for most accountants. He told me he was trying to find clients! As we were talking about our respective businesses, he asked me a series of questions. Our exchange went something like this:

"Bill, you use golf for business, don't you?"

"Sure, of course I do."

"I'm thinking about using golf more often. I want to use it as a means to get clients."

70

"Great idea, but if you want to play golf for work, I strongly recommend playing regularly. Don't be a once or twice a summer golfer. You need to make it a lifestyle choice and play every weekend. Find a group of guys who want to play every weekend and do it. Playing regularly is the only way to improve your game."

"Well, uh, thanks. But that's not what I want to know about golf."

"What do you want to know about golf?"

"When you play golf for business purposes...well...uh...what do you talk about?"

This was coming from someone who was no shrinking violet. He was an outgoing, engaging, funny, and very smart person. I thought his question was odd, then I realized, plenty of wannabe networkers probably have the same question.

What do I talk about?

I told him to talk about things people talk about. Be yourself. Talk about the game last night or that incredible rain storm last week or your crazy neighbor or that jackwagon politician, anything. Be yourself.

Don't! Set conditional meetings
Do not set up meetings and then add, "Let's confirm the day before." This demonstrates you don't value the other person's time. If you are going to set a meeting, actually set a meeting! The person you are maybe/possibly/not really sure if you want to/just might meet with may be running a tighter ship than you.

A person's calendar contains one very valuable commodity — time. If someone slots you into their calendar, that means they are eliminating that time slot for other people. Cancelling at the last minute leaves the other person with a hole in their day, a hole that they might have been able to fill with someone else.

Remember: networking is not about you; it's about the other person.

Do! Send your full contact info
I know, I know, everyone wants to be virtual these days. But when you set a time with someone, do that person a favor and include as much contact information as possible. Name, title, company, address, office phone, cell phone, email, etc. Your new contact may be using a CRM system that delineates between the various types of

phones. Providing your full contact information will help the other person properly record your pertinent information. This will come in handy if that other person needs to contact you in the future in order to give you something, say, a lead!

Do! Always provide your cell number

When setting meetings I always provide my cell number and I ask for the other person's cell number. Last minute changes happen and simply calling (or texting) someone to tell him you're running a few minutes late might be the difference between conducting a meeting vs. having the other person leave the meeting because he thinks you're not showing up.

Speaking of not showing up, as much as possible you should avoid cancelling a meeting at the last minute. When you agree to a meeting, that time slot is a very valuable commodity…for the other person. If you cancel the meeting the day before, the other person might have enough time to find a replacement, but given the short cancellation, that time slot might go unused. This is especially costly if someone is traveling to another city. A last minute cancellation means wasted time that could have otherwise been used to meet someone else.

Hierarchy of Networkers

In the networking world, some people are takers and some are givers. But that simple "taker vs. giver" dichotomy is not sufficient. The world of networking is comprised of many types of people. As a result, different techniques are appropriate at different times.

So with all due apologies to Maslow, here is my Hierarchy of Networkers.

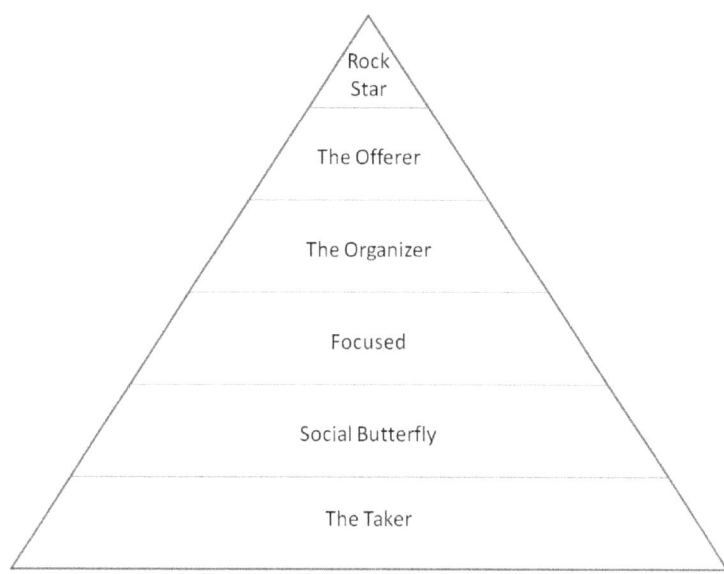

The Taker

The lowest form of networker is the taker. We've all dealt with is person. This is the person who "networks" with you solely to get something from you. "Who do you know who can help me?" and "I was told you might know a bunch of people who could be helpful to me" are common refrains heard from this person.

Oddly enough, takers are often experienced executives who suddenly find themselves out of work. Despite the accomplishments that lead them to an executive position, these people are often completely inept when trying to network and connect with others. Perhaps they have grown used to being in charge and having other people answer to them. Or perhaps, like so many accomplished people, they have a difficult time expressing their skills. If you have ever seen an out-of-work executive struggle to put together a cogent resume, you know what I mean.

Perfect for:
- Nobody. Don't be this person.

Social Butterfly

Networking begins when you know no one. If you are in this position, you need to do anything that puts you in a position to meet other people. Go to everything. Try to meet as many people as possible. Start building your networking base. In other words, this is the time when going to general networking events is valuable.

A general event is something that is open to the public. Anyone and everyone can attend. As a result, an ilk of people I call the professional networker shows up. These are people with little to offer and everything to gain. In other words, finding an actual client prospect at these events is a low probability. Everyone is trying to sell and very few are in a position to buy. These events are the dictionary definition of "networked to death."

However, being networked to death at this point in your career is not necessarily a bad idea. Today's connections with friends, competitors, and peers might be tomorrow's valuable Influencer. As you move up the networking hierarchy, these general events will have less and less relevance and use for your career. But when you're starting out, getting to know someone, anyone, can eventually prove to be valuable.

Perfect for:
- Recent college grads
- Associates and other entry-level or junior-level professionals
- People trying to restart their careers
- Job seekers without many contacts

Focused

The Focused networker spends her time networking with Influencers and Targets. She avoids the events frequented by social butterflies and instead has figured out where she can best find her Targets. She does everything possible to put herself in places where her Targets and Influencers frequent.

In order to accomplish this, she has spent time dissecting her industry and she has a thorough understanding of who sells to whom and who advises and helps those Targets.

The Focused Networker also understands the power of having something to offer and works diligently to find things of value she can offer those Targets and Influencers. Typical offers include meals, tickets to ball games and concerts, invitations parties and events, referrals, and so on. Please do not consider this list to be the end all be all of offers! Use your creativity when devising things you can offer your Targets and Influencers.

Perfect for:
- Mid-level professionals
- Sales professionals

The Organizer

The organizer does not merely wait for others to put together events that he can use to invite Targets and Influencers. He takes the initiative to organize those events. Instead of taking just one person to lunch or a ballgame, for example, the organizer will gather a small group of like-minded professionals.

Oddly enough, organizing events is relatively easy to do, yet very few others have the ability to do this. Some things the organizer can do include organizing outings to ballgames, lunches, informal happy hours, events to view NCAA tournament games, golf scrambles, and so. While movies and live theater are fine entertainment choices, they do not make good networking outings because people are not able to converse throughout the show.

Perfect for:
- Professionals moving through the ranks
- People looking to better leverage large contact bases

Great tip

A small group of thirty-something Chicago professionals have a "hamburger club." Instead of just getting together once a month for their networking meeting, the five members decided to find the best burger in Chicago. Each member was responsible for picking a burger joint and paying the evening's tab.

So instead of simply getting together to talk about mutual business opportunities (which can become boring and perfunctory), the group added a bit of adventure and something else to talk about instead of just business.

At the time of writing, the group is now on a quest to find the best barbeque joint in Chicago. You can organize a small group of (four to six) like-minded professionals and do the same thing. You can search for the best deli, Chinese, sushi, pizza, etc.

The Offerer

The offerer is the networker who has figured out what she can offer other people. While some offers are lunches and ball games and the like, the offerer has a unique talent or skill that other people value and enjoy. This might be writing, speaking, helping others, mentoring, investing in deals and so on.

The key to the offerer is others do not yet know she has something to offer. She constantly needs to market to other people. She needs to make sure she stays top of mind with others.

If you haven't figured out what you can offer, keep trying. Don't be dissuaded by failures. You'll figure it out. Eventually.

Perfect for:
- Creative types
- Senior professionals

Rock Star
At the top of the networking heap are those who are sought out by others. The rock star not only has something to offer others, others come to the rock star with offers. The rock star is in demand and quite often gets to pick and choose the best of the best offers. The rock star has a personal brand and that brand is in demand.

Who are the rock stars? The most obvious are celebrities (sports and entertainment figures, for example). These people get endorsement deals because of who they are and not because they asked to endorse basketball shoes. They have something to offer (fame, renown, notoriety) and that attribute is in demand and known to others.

Who else is a rock star? Anyone interested in buying a consumer good or a service. These are the opposite of the people trying to sell those things.

Perfect for:
- If you have to ask, you can't afford it.

Our economy is still based on free exchange
Remember that. If you are a newly minted college student or anyone trying to break in to a new career, remember to stop thinking about yourself. Think of the other person. I can't tell you how many times I've been contacted by college students who want to connect with me because of what I do for them. Typically, these overtures are gushing and fawning in nature and usually sound like this:

"I'd like to network with you and learn about how you got into investment banking. You have lots of experience and I am really, really interested in learning all about a great career and I know I will benefit from my time with you because you can teach me so much and I will learn and learn and learn all sorts of interesting bits of information that you painstaking learned on your own from years and years of experience and I, without investing anything, will be able to do a Vulcan mind meld and gain all of your knowledge. Whaddya say, old buddy old pal, wanna partake in this totally one-sided exchange where I get everything and you get nothing?"

I have no doubt these people are sincere, but most of these overtures lack any semblance of an idea of what I get out of the exchange. Here are some actual examples. Young people be warned, the approach these people used routinely lands them in the "do not respond" file…

"I came across your profile yesterday as I was doing lead gen for my company and am really fascinated by your background. Given your experience starting tech companies and also in the financial transactions space, I'd love to get together, pick your brain, and talk entrepreneurship (not a sales call). Are you free for coffee or lunch sometime next week?"

My response was simple: "That sounds like quite a bargain for you. What do I get out it?"

Here's another exchange:
"I'm looking for an M&A role at a middle-market investment bank and I want to learn more about your company, background, and any advice you have."

I decided to take mercy on this person and I actually responded. "What sort of role are you looking for…and why the heck would you want to do this?"

"I'm looking for an associate level role either on the buy or sell side. I want to do this because I have a passion for the markets and competition. I want work on deals and use my analytical skills to dive into transactions but still focus on the larger picture at hand. The best and brightest go into M&A and I want to be in an environment that constantly pushes me to improve my skills and to be the best."

As you might have guessed, I replied in my typical style: "Sounds like you've figured out what you get out of the bargain…have you figured out what the other guy gets?"

The Takeaway

The Condition: Novice networkers often fall into the trap of asking, née, demanding that other people do something for them. This is called the Passive Ask. The Passive Ask means you are asking someone else to do your job and if you ask someone to do your job for you, you will not get very far.

The Cure: Avoid the Passive Ask and focus on what you can offer others. If you develop a reputation as someone who helps others, makes referrals and opens doors for others, offers help to others, organizes events, and generally provides more than you take, you will find many, many doors will eventually open.

The Result: I'm executing my own plan! If you know me, you've probably be invited to events I've organized. I've probably offered you help or baseball tickets or insights. Or at least tried to offer you something. And this book you are reading is yet another piece of my offer puzzle.

Reader Homework: *I encourage you to build your own framework. Don't copy me. Do your own thing! Here are the questions you should ask yourself at this point:*
- Where are you on the hierarchy of networkers? Where do you want to be?
- Are you detail oriented when making introductions? Do you provide full contact information and a quick description of why you are making the introduction?
- Are you timely and consistent? Do you stick to your schedule or are you constantly cancelling meetings at the last minute?

Chapter 6

Real World Examples Cure Bad Networking

- You can't fix what's wrong until you understand what does not work and why it does not work.
- Asking is bad enough, but passively asking is even worse.
- Myopically seeking the perfect Target usually fails to provide anything of interest…to your Target

Being born again as a marketing minded person, I began to pay closer attention to websites, specifically, how companies describe their service offerings to the world. I'd look at the websites, often quite impressive with lots of fancy buzz words and slick graphics...and I couldn't figure out what the company did. I couldn't figure out who was supposed to respond to the site. And if I was interested in the ill-defined service offering, I couldn't figure out who I was supposed to contact.

Ironically, marketing/advertising companies seemed to be the worst culprits. These companies are not marketing to an end user. They are marketing to their fellow marketing/advertising companies. They know the competition will review their websites and they want to be impressive to their peers. The analogy I think is women getting dressed up on New Year's Eve. They don't get dressed up so much for their husbands and boyfriends, who rarely notice these things, they get dressed up for other women.

In other words...they are Networked to Death!

NTD Problems with Websites

Too many professional companies have websites that are afflicted with a form of NTD. In the desire to be impressive to their peers, they often unwittingly fail to communicate to their Targets. The complex messaging, the big words, the jargon do not connect with Targets — they are lay people in your industry — instead, the messaging is designed to connect with competitors. Companies do not want to seem simple and unsophisticated in the eyes of the competitors.

Worse, many sites lack a call to action. They lack a simple point of entry. A web developer friend of mine once pointed out a site he was developing for a private equity firm. The "about us" page had four bios of the principals. Each partner had a mug shot plus a recap of their impressive educations and lengthy backgrounds of success. The problem, my friend pointed out, is who do you contact? Two of the principals were in New York. A third was in Houston. And the fourth was in Idaho!

Websites, and vis-à-vis, marketing, often fail the rubber meets the road test. The fancy words, the impressive bios, the lack of a call to action all collude to create white noise. An impressive array of unactionable words and pictures.

Business development people are often buried on a website. If you want your business development people to connect with the outside world, shouldn't those business development people be front and center?

Yes, of course they should be front and center. They should be easy to contact. And if you want to earn extra credit, gold star, brownie points...give them titles other than "Director of Business Development."

NTD Problems with Job Titles

Professionals are guilty of creating job titles and descriptions based on internal interactions of the company. For example, we might think:

"Good Ol' Charlie is supposed to develop business, so I better call him VP of Business Development."

Ask yourself, when you've reviewed a website because you want to connect with a company, maybe even if you are seeking their services, do you instantly seek out the business development creature?

I don't. Most people don't. We want a decision maker. So why do we use "business development" to describe the people we want to connect with Targets? Silliness. Shouldn't job titles/descriptions be based on how we want the outside world (Targets) to interact with our people? The answer, of course, is YES!

If this still doesn't make sense, think of it this way. Let's say you're a top executive in a company, but you don't want to be bothered by pesky people calling you to sell you things or trying to buy things from you. Why do you place your mugshot, fancy title, and impressive bio front and center? You know you are going to be pestered, thus, you hire a crew of screeners to help prevent the great unwashed from actually connecting with you.

Instead, if you are a top executive and you do not want to be bothered by calls, your title should be "Director of SEO, IT, and Insurance Sales."

Nobody would call that person, right? So why do we insist on giving versions of that title to the very people we actually want to connect with our Targets?

NTD, that's why. We are not marketing to our Targets; we are marketing to our friends, competitors, and peers. We want to seem impressive when our neighbor checks out our website.

Rethink titles and job descriptions. Set up your organization so your intended Targets know who to contact.

NTD Problems with Pitches

If the messaging on the website is confusing, if our titles are not how our Targets want to think of us, guess what, our pitches in person might be off kilter. Shortly after I delivered my first NTD presentation, I had lunch with a consultant. He wanted to pick my brain about the merger & acquisition industry. He had some ideas about creating some software that would help investment bankers disseminate information and keep track of deals. We had a good conversation and he picked up the tab as a payment of sorts for tapping my expertise.

A few days later a dozen golf balls showed up at my office along with a nice note further expressing his gratitude. A classy move, to be sure. The balls had his company's name and logo on them, and as all lazy golfers know, we like logo balls because we don't have to put a mark on the ball to indicate it is ours. We love logo golf balls!

The next day I played a round and naturally used the new balls. As I was rapidly spraying those new balls all over the course, losing most of them, I began thinking about the logo. Anyone who found one of those balls would notice the logo and company name, but that person would have no idea what the company does. *What a waste of a marketing opportunity*, I thought.

As I reflected further, I figured professionals should be able to quickly and concisely explain what we do. Yes, I know this has been called the elevator pitch. While explaining a business concept in the length of time of a typical elevator ride (thirty seconds or so) is a good exercise, I think an even better idea is to explain what we do so concisely that it could fit on a golf ball. Blame the Internet Age and our increasingly shortened attention spans.

The idea of the Golf Ball Pitch is to accurately convey what you do in as short a time as possible. This might vary on the situation, of course. You'll probably never find the perfect Golf Ball Pitch. Instead, feel free to constantly refine and rework your Golf Ball Pitch.

So, what's my Golf Ball Pitch, you're probably asking. To answer that question, and to perhaps help you refine your Golf Ball pitch, let me take you through a couple of iterations of my pitch.

Bloated, full-on definition, utilizing industry jargon, impressive words, and complicated concepts

We are an investment bank serving middle-market business owners. We provide access to capital on both sides of balance sheet — equity, senior debt, mezzanine debt, and sundry hybrid instruments, such as unitraunche products. We also advise owners as they pursue transactions that involve the divestiture or conveyance of stock or assets in their companies, business units, product lines, and subsidiaries. We also undertake search functions for acquisition minded companies, helping to locate, contact, and eventually acquire suitable Targets.

This definition sounds impressive and is entirely accurate, but it is complicated and worse, it uses words that convey the wrong ideas. The main offender is "investment bank." People in my industry like that term because it sounds impressive: the term means a firm that is involved in underwriting, mergers & acquisitions, and other non-commercial bank activities. But when laypeople hear "investment" they immediately stop listening. They think my work involves personal investments, specifically the stock market. I have nothing to do with the stock market.

Quicker, to the point pitch, a.k.a., the "Elevator Pitch"

We help business owners sell their companies, acquire other companies, and raise capital for their companies. We work with middle-market companies, which we define as companies with annual revenues between $10 million to $300 million.

My elevator pitch is the one I use the most when I explain what I do. When speaking to people, I have more time available to me than when trying to write something on the side of a golf ball. But that exercise of trying to distill what I do to a golf ball sized definition is what helped me take a complicated, chunky explanation and make it as simple and direct as possible.

Golf Ball Pitch

Merger & Acquisition Specialists for Middle-Market Companies

Does this capture everything about what I do for a living? No, of course not, but it is not intended to do so. Instead, a few simple, well chosen words will help people quickly understand the gist of what I do and perhaps more importantly, what I *do not* do. Hopefully no one thinks I sell used cars or insurance or software or personal investment planning.

The Passive Ask

Marketing and networking errors, inconsistencies, omissions, and misguided messaging result in one thing: We force our people to ask. Asking is a problem because everyone else is asking. All that asking becomes background noise, eardrum buzz. Things get worse when professionals get a chance to interact with each other because they often employ something even worse than the ask; they use the "passive ask." The Passive Ask is when someone says, usually in a warbling, cracking voice, "If you have a client who needs what we do…think of us!"

And we wonder why we struggle to find clients.

PE World Example

Let me give you an example from my world, mergers and acquisitions (M&A). And lest I be guilty of using jargon and thus confusing the lay person, my work involves the buying and selling of companies. As you read this section, you may think I am picking on private equity and perhaps have a distain for it. I don't. Private equity plays a vital role in our economy and I often find myself empathizing with its denizens.

In the world of M&A the roles of buyer and seller are reversed. Selling a company is far easier than buying a company. The reason is because all buyers are offering the same thing — money. The dollars being offered by Buyer A are no different than the dollars being offered by Buyer B. The amounts, the terms, the timing of the offers may differ, but money is fungible.

Additionally, in the world of M&A, demand usually outstrips supply. Companies are almost always interested in making acquisitions and almost always *not* interested in being acquired. Unless a company is small and/or struggling, a company that is on the market will usually garner plenty of interest from buyers. So think about it, if a transaction closes, the seller has a 100% chance of being in that transaction, whereas the buyers have a far lower chance of crossing that finish line because in most M&A processes, more than one buyer expresses interest in doing a deal.

Buying companies is difficult because everyone wants to buy and everyone is offering the same thing.

Private equity (PE) firms exist for one reason only — to buy companies. They raise money from investors, called limited partners, and the PE firm is then supposed to deploy that money by making acquisitions. As described above, buying companies is difficult because everyone is doing it (or wants to do it). So what do many PE firms do to find acquisition Targets?

They unleash the newly minted MBA.

The newly minted MBA, as the name suggests, is someone who recently graduated from business school. These people are usually in their late twenties or early thirties. They are given the title of Something of Business Development.

Some of them previously held sales jobs and as a result, they have the scars that can result from the sales experience. And as anyone who has held a sales job will attest, we all dream of being on the other side — the buyer.

Now that the newly minted MBA is finished with their fancy MBA and they have a job that is on the buying side, they think they've landed on easy street.

Thank Elvis, the newly minted MBA thinks, I'm a buyer! This will be easy!

So the newly minted MBA begins his work. He calls companies and speaks to the owner. Or he attempts to speak to the owner because the newly minted MBA quickly discovers his overtures are rebuked before he can even make his pitch to the owner.

Holy moonpies, the newly minted MBA thinks, I think I'm still a seller. I'm offering money and money is a commodity and these owners seem to have heard my pitch many times. This work is difficult!

Finding an acquisition Target is difficult work. PE firms, while nominally a buyer, are in fact selling. They are selling themselves as a suitable partner for the owner because the asset they offer, money, is the same as the money offered by other firms.

The newly minted MBA is additionally hamstrung because they all tend to say the same thing: "We're different, we have money, we have industry experience...and we want to buy your company!" As savvy business owners who have been approached countless times know, the buy offer contains a caveat: "In a proprietary, non-competitive, underpriced, seller note, earn out sort of way."

The Eardrum Buzzsaw

When your messaging is the same as everyone else's, it is a form of the Passive Ask. PE messaging, in particular, becomes white noise to business owners. The asker is merely walking into an eardrum buzzsaw.

I saw the same thing when I spoke to a Harvard MBA class. The class was called "Entrepreneurship through Acquisition" and the class required students to engage business owners in conversations about buying businesses. Not as an exercise, but as a legitimate overture to buy the company. In other words, if the students hooked one, they were expected to reel it in.

I was on a panel of investment bankers brought in to give the students some real world feedback about buying and selling companies. During lunch prior to the class, the two professors who ran the class gave us the lowdown on the students. The students were all high achievers and, as we would certainly discover, all highly intelligent. They were tops of their classes in high school, had every college literally begging them to attend, aced college and had their pick of job offers upon graduation. When they decided to go to business school, they all experienced the same thing — they were all in demand and could pick where they wanted to go.

Upon walking into "Entrepreneurship through Acquisition," this hot streak of being wanted was about to come to a sudden, shocking stop for these high achievers. For the first time in many of their lives, one of the professors explained, the students faced rejection. They experienced failure.

The business owners called by these students — surprise, surprise — didn't give a hoot and they cared even less when they learned the caller was a Harvard student.

As I sat in front of the class, my first observation about the students was they were all whip smart. Not a surprise, this was Harvard after all. Bright, eager, prepared, outgoing. A great class. My second observation about the class, which unfolded during our session, was they were guilty of myopia.

"So, your teachers told me you all had an assignment..." I paused for moment and scanned the room. The students' body language changed as they suddenly realized I was about to bring up the bad thing.

FAILURE! Holy crap, I failed at something! And this guy knows!

As the students shrunk back into the seats, I asked them what they thought of the exercise. Numerous frustrating stories emerged as the students relayed setback after setback. Since they were all highly intelligent, I didn't have to tell them anything further. They knew. Buying a business is a very difficult thing.

Myopia Results in Quixotic Pursuit of Perfection
I asked the Harvard students about their approaches. Without exception, their approaches were all a form of the Ask. They simply asked the owners what those owners had heard countless times before. As I also discovered, the students' approaches were myopic.

They took a lot of time to perfectly define a perfect Target and why that perfect Target was so perfect for themselves. Typically, these traits of a "perfect for me" acquisition Target were:
- High growth
- Fat profit margins
- No customer concentration
- Barriers to entry/defensible market position
- Owner willing to sell at a low price

As the other investment bankers and I pointed out, these sound like great companies, so why would someone be willing to sell a great thing at a low price to a complete stranger who merely made one cold call?

I told the students they needed to find a hook. Something different from all the other Asks that were lobbed at the business owners. They need to have a thesis, a plan, an idea, something, anything that would enable them to have a conversation with the owner. Only then might they be able to move forward and make an offer to a willing counterpart.

As the students reflected on my comment, they naturally asked, "What can we do to stand out? How can we be different?"

I told them what I tell everyone who asks that question. I can't do everything for you; you have to figure out some things on your own!

As the students struggled with ways to differentiate themselves, one asked, "Should we tell them we go to Harvard?"

You can imagine the response from the panel.

The Antidotes to NTD
I've explained a few situations, so let's explore some solutions...

Personnel

How we view our employees and how our sales Targets and clients view our employees are often very different. We tend to give our employees titles and job descriptions that make sense to the leaders of the firm. In reality, the messaging from titles/job descriptions should fit the intended Target.

Don't be afraid of being creative. Don't be afraid of being different. Do you really think you stand a better chance of winning business with yet another pleasant, intelligent, but otherwise nondescript person with the title of Director of Business Development?

While writing this book I had breakfast with a Director of Business Development for a mid-sized accounting firm. I almost cancelled the meeting because I thought I was about to meet with yet another earnest but utterly indistinguishable "Something of Business Development."

I have a problem with titles that include "business development." I think most business owners do as well. Business Development has a connotation of young and/or inexperienced people dialing for dollars. And in practical terms, business development personnel tend to be the ones who order the sandwiches for the meetings with prospects. The senior people show up and do the real selling. Because of that reality, business development people should really be renamed: Expensive Cold Calling Sandwich Orderers.

I am very happy I stayed the course and took the meeting. Instead of a twenty something saying the exact same things in the exact same ways as everyone else, my breakfast mate was a highly experienced business operator. He started in public accounting but after a few years, he segued into business ownership. With a couple of other partners, he raised some money from some wealthy families and bought and ran over a half dozen companies. He peppered his verbal biography with interesting anecdotes that could only come from someone who has bought, run, and sold companies.

He relayed all of this in about four minutes at the start of the meeting. When he finished, I told him one thing, "You have the wrong title."

In his job he is supposed to connect with business owners for the purpose of determining if the company needs a service his company offers. I told him, "Why not do something different? Call yourself 'God-Guru of Middle-Market Business Experience' or something suitably different and off the wall and descriptive of your experience and insights?"

The conversation my breakfast mate could have with business owners is far different than that of a twenty-five-year-old. Why not leverage that experience and those insights? Why not do something different so when you contact a wary business owner, you actually stand out from the masses of business development creatures doing and saying the same things?

I mean, you wouldn't want to do something silly such as actually connect with business owners and sell them your services, would you?

Lessons: Find sales people with a suitable level of senior experience. Free them to be unique and different. Set them up so sales Targets can quickly discern they have insights and talents far beyond the usual bill of fare served up by younger business development people.

In other words, find the right people and the right words to describe those people so your sales Targets will want to interact with them. If you don't, your business development people are liable to be little more than expensive sandwich orderers.

Point of Entry
Websites should work to lead visitors to the right people. Go to your website, how easy is it for visitors to figure out with whom they should interact?

While writing this book I was cold called by a business development creature from a very large, very successful west coast private equity firm. As I pulled up the website and tried to find her bio, she proceeded to explain why her firm was different...by saying all the same things as every other PE firm. Unfortunately, I was unable to find her bio. However, I was able to find the very impressive bio of the very impressive founder.

I was able to easily find the bio of the founder because it was front and center, easy to find. Anyone who gazed upon his extraordinary accomplishments would be left suitably impressed. Clearly, this guy was über connected and über experienced. This is the guy with whom everyone would want to speak.

Unfortunately, his contact information was nowhere to be found. No phone number, no email. I could only think of one reason why his impressive bio was "front and center" in the website. He wanted

90

to impress his friends, neighbors, and competing private equity firms.

Worse, the business development people at the firm were buried deep inside the website. I had to hunt and peck, then scroll to the bottom of a long page, where I found a couple of rather puny bios (and no pictures) of the handful of business development creatures employed by this private equity firm to connect with business owners for the purpose of developing opportunities!

Talk about being Networked to Death! This PE firm wasn't set up to interact with business owners (or investment bankers who might have a client who would be a suitable acquisition Target for the fund). Instead, this PE firm was set up to interact with friends, competitors, and peers.

The antidote for this is simple. Your marketing efforts and online presence should be aimed at your Target, not your peers and competitors. If necessary, reconfigure your website to give visitors a simple and precise path to connect with the person you want them to connect with. Being a marketing focused company might mean checking your ego at the door and placing your sales people (with appropriate/better/interesting titles) front and center.

If you are a top executive and you don't want to connect with people, consider taking your bio off the website. If you are a lowly business development creature and your company refuses to rework your title, description, and website placement...consider finding a new employer.

Messaging
Saying and writing the same thing in the same way as everyone else will typically result in one thing — white noise. Instead, cut down on the jargon and buzzwords and simplify your messaging so your intended Target can understand it. Remember, they are not in your business; they are not experts in your industry.

Instead, write so your mother or a child will quickly and easily "get it." Who cares if your peers and competitors think you're a simpleton if you are connecting with your Target and winning business? Find a thesis. Find something interesting to talk about. Take the time to get to know people.

The Takeaway

The Condition: Failure to connect with Targets due to overly focusing on yourself. This is also known as myopia.

The Cure: The lesson we should all take from this exercise is the seeker of the "perfect for me" Target rarely spends time communicating what the Target gets from the bargain. If you want to connect with a sales Target, an employer, a mentor, a referral source, stop thinking about what you get out of the exchange and think about what you can offer the other person.

The Result: When you stop thinking about yourself and figure out what you can do for the other person, you will be surprised at the doors that will open.

Reader Homework: I encourage you to build your own framework. Don't copy me. Do your own thing! Here are the questions you should ask yourself at this point:

- Describe what you do in as few words as possible. How quickly can you accurately convey your work to other people?
- Do you regularly employ the passive ask when meeting with people?
- Do your website and marketing materials make finding your sales people difficult or easy?
- Do you have "business development" anywhere in your title? Is that the person your Targets want to find? Or would a different title make more sense?
- Are you describing the perfect client for you? Or are you demonstrating what you can do for them?

Chapter 7

Creating Goals Cures Bad Networking

- Setting goals and executing a plan are the only ways you will be able to connect with others in a manner that is meaningful for your career.
- Self-publishing is a great technique to build credibility. It gives you something to talk about and it may help open further doors.

Now that (hopefully) I've pounded the notion of being different and finding a hook, let's talk about how you can implement that into your marketing efforts. Oh, wait a minute. I have no idea what you do and given the fact people from a multitude of different industries will be reading this book, I am unable to provide you with any specific help.

Instead, in this section I provide some of my goals and processes to differentiate myself, foster creativity, and stand apart from the crowd. While this section is about my marketing and networking goals, I hope readers of all types will be able to utilize my approaches, specifically:

- For executives and team leaders — I hope you find a few tidbits that you can use to help your people differentiate and perhaps develop personal brands.
- For individuals trying to further their careers — don't wait for the world to bestow a tile on you. Claim expertise in something but be able to back up those claims.
- And for job seekers — you need to find something you can offer employers other than, "Hire me, pay me, and I'll do work for you."

My Networking Development Goals

1. Learn How You Learn — Once you learn how you learn, you will have a much easier time feeding yourself information/experiences in the ways you best absorb that information. Is your learning preference reading, writing, visual, auditory, kinesthetic?
2. Be Memorable — don't be afraid of being different, of having a personality, of being a character. Find a way to differentiate yourself because you'll never stand out if you strive to be the best at fitting in. Being presentable and professional at the cost of being just like everyone else will yield you nothing. You won't be remembered.
3. Be Knowledgeable — being memorable means little if you're not knowledgeable. You don't want to be known as a wiseacre know-nothing. Do your homework, study, prepare. Find a skill that few others have, develop that skill, tout that skill, become an expert. While you don't have to wait until the world calls you an expert on something, you better be able to back up your claims.
4. Get It Done — the world is full of talkers. But very few accomplish what they say they're going to do. If you say you're going to do something, follow through and see it to the end.

5. Be Approachable & Genuine — being open, gregarious, funny, quick, honest are the traits that will connect you with others.
6. Experience All You Can — that is the path to being able to find insights. Don't be afraid of trying new things. In fact, get out of your comfort zone. One of the reasons I accepted the offer to write a book was to get out of my comfort zone. As odd as it may sound, part of my brain still thinks ten written pages is a massive undertaking.
7. Be Honest and Trustworthy — this should go without saying, but this basic "golden rule" admonishment is often overlooked and forgotten as people advance in their careers. You should never have to say you are honest and trustworthy — those traits should be apparent. A lesson my father taught me years ago was something some wise old sage taught him long before I was born...you can trust 5% of the people you meet explicitly. The other 95%? You watch like a hawk. You want to be in that 5%.
8. Speak Your Mind — being memorable means being someone who is direct and says things that might be uncomfortable for others, but if at all possible, find a way to soften the blow.
9. Be Adaptable — life is not a set plan as much as it is it an exercise of driving by feel. Yes, make plans and set goals but you also need to remain open to making adjustments as you learn and experience more.
10. Truly understand your strengths and weaknesses — tout your strengths or find team members who shore up your weaknesses. Avoid giving advice in areas where you are weak. Defer, learn, and take other people's advice. Business bogs down when those who are not experts are proffering their opinions on subjects where they just don't know what the heck they're talking about.
11. Have fun and enjoy your work — truly enjoying what you do will eventually increase the odds of success.

My Marketing Plan

I use my book, *Mergers & Acquisitions For Dummies*, as a unique "leave behind." The book is a third party validation and helps me quickly prove my bona fides to others. I also try to write and speak as much as possible. I've do regular newsletters, write articles and books, and I speak at universities and professional groups. The world can be your podium and I want to be in a position to connect with as many people as possible.

Business owners are the usual purchasers of my services, so I obviously want to connect with them. To get to business owners, I often have to be referred by Influencers. In my industry, those Influencers are wealth managers, lawyers, accountants, and commercial bankers. While I want to connect with all of those people, I want to go beyond relying on the Passive Ask. I try to find something I can offer all of them. I try to understand their challenges connecting with prospects and winning business.

I don't waste my time with *de facto* events (peers & competitors). My industry, like most other industries, is full of various professional organizations and groups. While many of these groups are fine organizations populated with diligent, professional people, the problem I have with industry groups is they are filled with either my peers (other investment bankers) or people I have no problem contacting (private equity firms). What the professional organizations lack is the constituency I want to meet — business owners and executives.

I set up a couple of "Networking Days" every week. I have standard meeting times and I meet with a select group of trusted professionals. I want to stay on their radar for when they might be able to refer leads to me and as much as I can, I like to refer leads to them.

I use sporting events and casual cocktail networking events (that I organize) as further marketing touch points. I send out occasional emails to my trusted adviser group (see appendix B for some examples). And of course...golf.

As of this writing, areas where I need to improve are website, social media, and better consistency in my writing. Please see appendix A for a deeper dive into my marketing plan.

My Personal Brand

My personal brand is a writer, speaker, optimist, connector of people, and conveyor of value. I called myself the accidental marketer but I am diligently working on reducing the accidents. For a short while, I thought I wanted to call myself a "thought leader," but after I saw how many people on LinkedIn call themselves "thought leader," I've had a change of heart. I now believe people should not be allowed to use "thought leader" to describe themselves unless they can think of another term for "thought leader."

The World is Your Podium: Self-Publishing Tips

The world offers you an array of tools and programs that you can use for little or no expense. Self-publishing is one of those tools. As I've describe in this book, I can trace an inflection point in my career to the point in 2003 when I self published a book.

I went to college in 1985. I hauled a typewriter with me. The technology in my dorm room was similar to all other dorm rooms for the time: A telephone, a TV that picked up six or seven channels, a radio, a typewriter, and a stereo that played LPs and cassettes. I laugh when I think about how we thought we were at the cutting edge of human evolution.

When that student of the 80s sat in his dorm room, he was utterly, totally, and completely cut off from the world. Sure, if you had connections, or if were able to put yourself in the right place, you might find yourself in a position to publish or record music. When I think back to, say, 1987, I realize how isolated we were. Sure, we had social circles and went to parties and ball games and so forth, but our worlds were small. Someone who wrote a great book would have a very difficult time fighting through all the clutter of a world asking.

And when you think about it, technology wasn't that different in the 80s as compared to the 50s when my parents were in college.

Today, a student sitting in the same room has at the tip of his fingers the entire world. I marvel at those opportunities. I got my first taste of this in 2003 as people from around the world contacted me. Corresponding with people from Israel, South Africa, Russia, Japan, Australian, Norway, the UK, Canada, Argentina, and many, many more, was now part of my normal day.

I encourage anyone who wants to stand out from the crowd to write and self-publish a book. In fact, take a look at My Networking Development Goals (above). So let's see how well I did:

1. Learn how you learn – I learn by experiencing then writing about those experiences
2. Be Memorable, don't be afraid of being different – I wrote a book about venture capital that claimed to use Keith Richard's guitar tuning from "Brown Sugar" as a paradigm for venture capital.
3. Be Knowledgeable – I demonstrated the depth of my understanding about venture capital and did so in an easy to understand way
4. Get it done – I worked on it until it was complete
5. Be Approachable & Genuine – I took a rather obtuse subject and wrote a simple, straight forward, and often humorous book about the subject.
6. Experience All You Can – I was able to draw upon my experiences of working for companies funded by friends & family, angels, venture capitalists, and the public markets.

7. Be Honest and Trustworthy – I can only hope my readers found my advice and insights to be honest and trustworthy
8. Speak Your Mind – I was unafraid to take some chances and have some fun in my writing.
9. Be Adaptable – Even as I write this book I have adapted and changed and updated my techniques. I will continue to do so for the rest of my life. You need to keep what works, but more importantly, you need to get rid of the things that don't work.
10. Truly understand your strengths and weaknesses – one of my strengths is writing and without really thinking about it, writing a book on venture capital allowed me to tout that skill.
11. Have fun and enjoy your work – I had a blast writing the book and I've been constantly surprised and delighted at the results.

The Title
The first rule to self-publishing is to find a descriptive title. *Venture Capital 101* was a bit of dumb luck. I can't say I did much thinking about it. It was the first thing that popped into my mind as I was writing. To this day, if you search "venture capital" on Amazon, my book is one of the top results. Why? Because people seeking to learn about venture capital are probably using "venture" and "capital" as search terms!

Forget Paper — Use Electricity
The second rule is to eschew paper. You can self-publish and reach the world without ever having to produce a single paper copy of your work. The fact you're reading this book is proof of that (review the *Venture Capital 101* parts again in case you've forgotten).

In the days before the Internet, a book meant paper, ink, glue, bindings, dust jackets, and in the days before computers, typesetting. Publishing a book meant incurring thousands of dollars of materials cost in addition to the cost of editors, proofreaders, and, of course, the author's time.

After the book was finished, additional costs included shipping, storage, returns, and sales and marketing expenses. For the self-published author with no discernible market nor any product placement on retailers' shelves, a self-published book often meant tens of thousands of dollars of expense and a car in the driveway. After all, those copies of the book had to go somewhere, and they often ended up in the garage collecting dust.

Printers do not care if your book sells. I'm sure they would prefer authors of self-published titles to find success, but the fact is printers are in the business to print. If you place an order, they are only too happy to take your money. Just because you hire someone to do work for you does not mean you will be successful because of that work.

You can publish a book these days without the need for paper, ink...or publishers, for that matter. The Internet and computer programs are the great levelers of our times. In addition to eliminating the costs of paper, ink, bindings, glue, etc., the Internet neatly handles another problem that plagued self-published authors — access to the world.

Options to disseminate your electronic book include Amazon, Lulu, iTunes, and other sites. If you really, really, really want to have paper copies of your book, of course, you can still hire a bookmaker to print up copies of your book — printers are happy to take your money. You can also utilize services such as CreateSpace to print physical copies.

The Magic Price Point: 99 Cents
When I placed *Venture Capital 101* for sale through Kindle Digital Press I had the option of pricing the book at any price I wanted. At the time (winter 2011) Amazon offered a couple of pricing options: 1) 70% for books priced at five dollars or more, and 2) 35% for books priced less than five dollars.

I wasn't hoping or planning for big sales. Since my "real" book was set to be published in the spring of 2011, my only goal was to use Amazon as a repository of my earlier work. I did not expect to sell many copies and I certainly harbored no illusions about making a fortune.

So I set the price point at the lowest price that enabled me to earn the highest commission rate. At five dollars I usually sold 1 or 2 or 3 copies per month. Frankly, I was amazed that anyone found the title and even more amazed they were willing to plunk down some money to buy it! While I was proud of the book, the title was eight years old at that point.

Over the next few months, I began paying more attention to articles about self-publishing, and by the end of 2011, I had read enough to rethink my pricing strategy. The theory behind the 99 cent price point is people are willing to take a gamble on a completely unknown item with a dollar. "If the book stinks," so goes the theory, "I've only wasted a dollar." Anything more than dollar and seems like real money.

Over the next few months I was surprised at what happened. I sold 20 copies in a month, then 30, then 50, then 80, then 100, and then 120. And sometimes even more.

Granted, this is small potatoes. In a typical month I usually earn between $30 and $50. For me, the key wasn't the money, it was the fact that hundreds of people from all over the world were buying by title every year.This was proof of concept for me that the right price, even absent a marketing strategy, could help me connect with a wider audience.

As of summer 2014, if you search "venture capital" in Amazon, my title is often the number one search item. If not number one, it is usually in the top three.

Get a Graphics Person to Design the Cover
The third rule is to have an eye catching cover. Or at a minimum,

have a cover that doesn't cause harm to your work. As I mentioned earlier, I have no design skills, so cover design is a challenge for me. Fortunately, a friend took mercy on me and created a simple and clean cover. It should be nearby.

Back in the dark ages, I worked in the video retailing industry as a district manager. I received preorder details of the titles that were being sent to my stores. I was unfamiliar with most of the titles because of a simple reason — most films at that time (mid 90s) were of the straight to video variety. They never played at theaters and as a result, were not reviewed and received little to no promotional support.

So how did these unknown movies, often starring unknown actors, gain traction with the customer. The cover box! Put a pretty girl on the cover of an unknown movie and — Voilà! — the title flew out door!

Similar to the visual marketing of unknown movies starring unknown actors, the unknown author of an unknown book needs something visual to help people take a look at the item.

While I am not suggesting putting pretty girls on a cover merely to garner sales, a modicum of professionalism can be a boon to sales.

You want a connotation of the product you're selling. If it's a cheesy movie filled with eye candy, you put a pretty girl on the cover. If it is a business oriented book, have a cover that connotes the contents of the book.

Work with an editor and proofreader
One of the huge benefits of working with a publisher is they provide an editor and a proofreader. No matter the talent and skill of the writer, everyone needs an editor. And after you and your editor are through beating each other up, you will both need a proofreader.

A good editor can help you refine and clarify your message and simplify and condense your writing. I also cite the prototypical "reduce three sentences into two" as one of major benefits a good editor can bring to your project. A fresh set of eyes quickly can spot redundancy in your writing.

No matter how much you try, your writing will have typos. When I wrote *Venture Capital 101,* I used the word "magnet" when I meant "magnate." I recall getting a snarky email from someone who pointed out this mistake. One of the downsides to spell check technology is it won't pick errors such as that. Someone with an even fresher set of eyes than your editor will spot those errors in a heartbeat.

And no matter how much you try, a written work of length will have typos. Do the best you can then don't worry about it. One of the great things about electronic books is when you discover the inevitable typos, you can fix them quickly.

Fire up your marketing machine
If you get lucky and get a chance to write a book for a publisher, you discover something — the marketing of the book is left to the author. Notable exceptions are books written by well-known, famous people such as politicians, sports figures, business leaders, and famous authors.

For those well-known authors, a book deal might include a marketing program, which probably entails a team that will set up TV and radio interviews, garner print and online reviews, and set up speaking engagements. For the rest of us, those tasks are left in the hands of the author.

In the past, a book deal with a publisher meant product placement on retail shelves. This was an enormous benefit but with the advent of Internet the self-published author now as entrée to the entire world. Frankly, I marvel at our ability to connect with the world.

I highly recommend using Amazon to sell your book. You can also use other sites such as iTunes and Lulu. Make sure you set up an author's page so potential buyers can learn more about you and your work. Set up a fan page on Facebook and list your book in the publications section on your LinkedIn profile.

Twitter is a great way to generate buzz and attention. Send tweets using a hash tag (#) to highlight relevant search terms.

And if you really want to get crazy, hire a publicist to help you perform all of these tasks.

After you release your book, you will be asked two questions: how many copies have you sold and can I have a free copy? I always get a kick out of people who ask the sales question. They usually have no basis of understanding books sales, and if you tell the person you've sold 1,000 or 10,000 or 500 of 25,000 copies, do those numbers mean anything to the person? Prior to writing a book for a publisher, I was in the same boat.

Aggregate sales do not provide a viable assessment of a book's performance. Instead, you want to pay attention to the velocity of sales. Amazon posts a book's sales rank and if a title is consistently in a range of about 20,000 to 100,000 that means the title is probably selling about 100 to 200 titles per month. When you see a best seller's rank with seven digits, that probably means the book sells a copy every few months.

The result
On the next page you will see an Amazon search of "venture capital" from April 2015... twelve years after I initially released this title to the world. Because of the confluence of descriptive title and low price point, my little venture capital tome is the first search result that shows up.

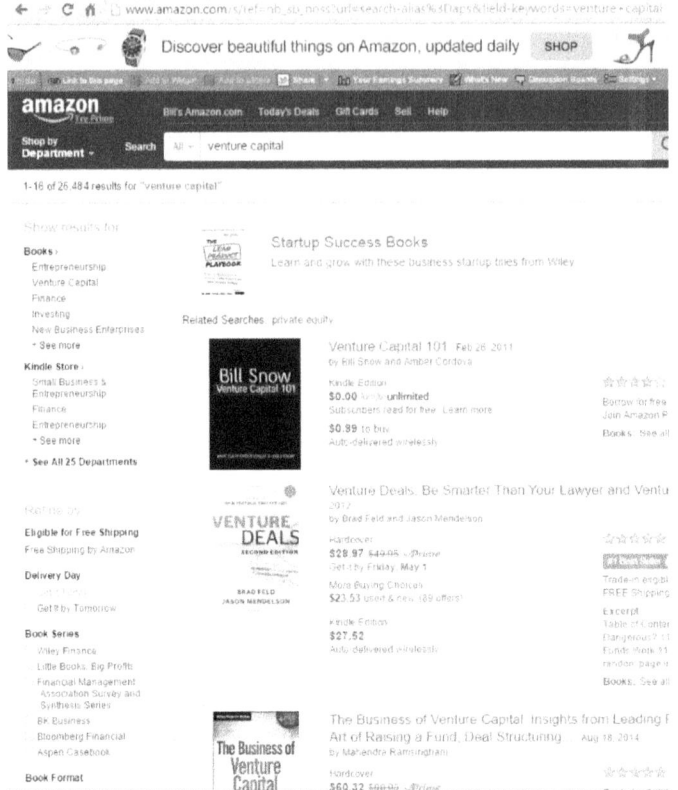

The Takeaway

The Condition: Networking without a plan or a purpose. Randomly meeting people and hoping brief interludes with strangers turn into a career or a sale.

The Cure: Your odds of meeting and connecting with other people who might help you are improved if you have goals, a plan, and a personal brand. Figure out a personal marketing plan based on your personality and your industry. What are you good at, what do you enjoy? Utilize your skills and talents in a directed and planned manner, to broaden your network.

The Result: I've tailored a marketing plan based on my strengthens — writing, connecting, thinking — and while I've tweaked and changed it over the years, I continue to move forward and execute my plan that is largely based on my personal brand. In fact, this book you are reading right now is part of that plan.

Reader Homework: *I encourage you to build your own framework. Don't copy me. Do your own thing! Here are the questions you should ask yourself at this point:*
- Have you figured out what you are good at?
- Have you figured out your skills?
- If you do not enjoy what you do for a living, what steps are you taking to remedy that situation?
- What is your personal brand?

Chapter 8

The End. Finally

When I think about the people who are successful at networking, and by extension, in their careers, five key traits come to mind. I call them the Five "Bees":

1. Be active – The last person who walks past the door often is the one who gets asked to enter.
2. Be memorable – Don't be afraid of standing out from the crowd. This will further increase your odds of being asked to enter.
3. Be knowledgeable – You won't be able to close deals unless you know what you are talking about.
4. Be professional – Having a personality is imperative, but it should not come at the expense of your professionalism.
5. Be honest – Activity and differentiation will go for naught unless you can back them up with skill, insights, and ethics.

Important Networking Tactics
The Five "Bees" are useless unless you have some specific tactics. Those tactics are:

Know what you're getting into before doing it
- Avoid "networking" events with friends, competitors, and peers as they are neither Targets nor Influencers.

Network with whom you want to do business
- Spend time with your Targets or Influencers to Targets.

Develop marketing that thinks of the other side
- Stop asking, start offering.
- Do favors and open doors for others.

Avoid myopic, quixotic pursuit of clients perfect for you
- Understand Targets'/Influencers' sales processes and challenges.
- Find ways to help them connect with their Targets.

Truly understand your strengths and weaknesses
- Encourage all of your people to undertake the same self-analysis.
- Shore up your weaknesses by finding team members who complement (not duplicate) your strengths.

Learn how you learn
- Learn how your employees learn – reading, writing, visual, auditory, kinesthetic – and deliver messages in the way each individual absorbs messages.

Encourage your people to build personal brands
- Jump at every opportunity (speaking, panels, writing, etc.)
- Utilize the modern tools: Facebook, LinkedIn, Twitter, Udemy, Google+.
- Jump into the self-publishing world: Amazon Digital Press, Lulu, iTunes and myriads of other services offer us all a great way to differentiate ourselves.

Don't wait for the world to bestow a title
- Encourage your people to find their unique talent, the thing (other than what they're selling) that they can offer to others.
- Don't wait for the world to proclaim you're an expert, call yourself one, but make sure you are prepared and knowledgeable. Do your homework!

Be genuine, be honest
- Avoid putting on airs, being "fake."
- Provide direct answers to direct questions.
- Tell the truth and not what you *think* the other person wants to hear.
- Speak from your heart, don't worry about offending — no matter what you do, you're going to tick off someone.

Brevity/lean content/KISS
- Encourage your people to distill their pitch to as small a space as possible. Your goal is to so quickly and accurately define what you do that if someone picked up a golf ball with your description they would immediately know what you do.

Don't be afraid of being different or memorable
- You want Targets and Influencers to immediately be able to remember your people.
- If you do things like everyone else, expect the same results as everyone else.
- You'll never stand out if you strive to be the best at fitting in.

Bill, what can I offer?
Whenever I've talked to people about avoiding the Passive Ask and finding something to offer, they often ask me the same question, "What can I offer?"

I always say the same thing. You have to figure that out for yourself, I can't do everything for you!

And the same is true for you, gentle reader; you need to figure out what you can offer. This book was designed only to show you some insights and get you thinking about a different framework for going about your professional life. Only you can figure out what you can offer someone else.

If you and your people can avoid being "Networked to Death" you and your people will be able to convey value to other people. Offering something of value (instead of asking for something) means people will be more apt to meet with you and better yet, people will contact you and offer you things. More doors will open for you, you'll be able to move forward until you face another door, and the process is repeated.

And maybe, just maybe, if you are good enough at this, you'll be invited to speak to networking groups and get a chance to write a book!

What You Can Offer (Me)

1. If you liked the book, please connect with me via LinkedIn and give me a recommendation:
   http://www.linkedin.com/in/billsnow
2. Send me a sleeve (preferably a dozen) of golf balls with your logo, I'll post a picture of it on my site. Remember, your logo/tag line should be enough for people to figure out what you do and contact you. Send me an email for my mailing address, bill@billsnow.com
3. Hire me to speak at your event, group, or company. You can contact me at bill@billsnow.com

Appendix A
Marketing Brief

A Marketing Company that does M&A
By Bill Snow

Preamble

In August 2010, after a two-year "on again, off again" discussion with Wiley Publishing, I signed a contract to write *Mergers & Acquisitions For Dummies*. I wrote the book between Labor Day and Christmas 2010, it was edited and proofed during winter 2011, and released in May 2011.

I received a copy of the book in late April 2011, shortly before the official release date. I remember being excited and proud of my accomplishment. That excitement lasted only a few seconds before I began to think, "Big deal...what do I do with it?" I was so focused on conceptualizing the book, plotting the flow of information, and of course, doing the actual writing, that I completely overlooked the marketing aspect of the book. Frankly, I just didn't think about it.

As I reflected on how I could market the book, and more importantly, how the book could be used as a part of a marketing plan for M&A advisory services, I undertook a rather intensive review of my strengths and weakness. And through trial and error, I began to create and execute a marketing plan for M&A advisory work.

A big part of this development was being invited to speak to the University Club's professional networking group about my experiences with networking, marketing, book writing, and differentiation. I called that presentation "(How to Avoid Being) Networked to Death." The subtitle of that presentation was, "or how I became an accidental marketer and ended up talking to you today."

I am very much an "accidental marketer." My M&A experience has been on the execution and materials preparation side of the ledger. But I think my expertise as an execution person provides insights that are not found in people who have never worked an M&A deal. I approach my work with the eye of deal person, not a business development person.

I also think having an operational background and not a twenty or thirty-year history as a business development person has allowed me to look at the issue of M&A advisory marketing with a fresh set of eyes. The following brief contains the insights and ideas garnered from being an execution person.

Goal

To help create the number one middle-market investment bank in the Chicago area and to be consistently on the tip of the tongue of referral sources. This will be accomplished through a multi-pronged marketing plan that consistently generates new leads but also helps convert old, "radio silent" leads.

Reality

Most, if not all, middle-market M&A advisory firms do good work, have good people, and they all claim to be (or want to be thought of as) the top firm. However, high quality work is systemic in the M&A advisory industry and therefore attempting to differentiate by passively hoping referral sources think of the firm as being substantially better than others is not realistic.

Instead, the focus should be on being memorable, knowledgeable, professional, approachable, and most of all...top of mind for referral sources. And being top of mind comes from consistent messaging and a multi-pronged marketing plan.

Concrete vs. Fuzzy Sales

When I use the term "concrete sales," I do not mean literally selling a coarse granular material embedded in cement. I refer to a sales cycle 1) that has a sense of urgency, and 2) where a decision to hire a firm will occur. Business valuation work is very much a concrete sale.

Valuations are triggered by another event: a death, divorce, annual review, etc. The work must be performed. Since multiple firms usually make a pitch to the prospect, I call this "bake off city." A decision will be made but only one firm will win the valuation mandate.

The mistake that most of us in the M&A advisory industry make is to consider other firms to be our number one competitors. We like to think we are in bake offs where a decision will be made — and sometimes we are in those situations — but more often, our top competitors are no decision, radio silence, and stasis.

Think about your past prospects. How many of them hired other firms? How many just faded away? If your prospect funnel is similar to mine, I suspect most of those leads simply never made a decision.

I consider M&A advisory to be in the world of fuzzy sales. Prospects often have no sense of urgency to make a decision to move forward with an M&A advisor, and as a result, prospects simply refrain from making a decision to engage any firm. Instead, M&A advisors get stuck in the endless cycles of "call me after the holidays, call me when the weather warms up, call me after the summer, call me after I take my kid to school, call me after the holidays."

My techniques are designed to provide multiple touch points and consistent messaging and branding. They are designed to be a technique to communicate to those who have gone "radio silent." My goal is to create a sense of urgency and help remove prospects from the world of stasis.

Targets
The target markets for my marketing are twofold: 1) Referral sources (lawyers, accountants, wealth managers, commercial bankers), and 2) prospects.

Stasis Marketing: Offers not Asks
As much as possible, I focus on the "offer" instead of the "ask." For example, asking a prospect to meet to talk about their M&A options is an "ask." Inviting the prospect to an event is an "offer." Reminding a referral source to "think of us when you have a client in need of our services" is an ask. Inquiring about their interest in participating in an event is an offer.

Offers tend to cut through the clutter of countless asks. That said, asking for the business is entirely appropriate and I am not suggesting we abandon the ask. Instead, focusing on offers puts us in a much better position to eventually move to the ask.

The goal of my marketing is to find something to offer every group with which we interact. Lawyers, accountants, and wealth managers can be offered participation in business owner events. Not only does this put them in contact with business owners/executives, it allows them to market the event to their prospects, thus allowing them to offer something instead of asking for something.

Commercial banking is a commodity and differentiation is extremely difficult. For this group I am offering my "Networked to Death" presentation. I give this presentation gratis and even tell them I won't talk about my work (M&A) unless an attendee asks.

Commercial bankers can stand out from the herd by inviting their prospects (and clients) to an event to hear some interesting, funny, and insightful observations about marketing, networking, and differentiation.

While I refrain from the "hard sell" during these presentations, I'm also assuming if I can get in front of enough business owners, eventually some will turn into prospects and clients. I also assume if I provide a service for commercial bankers, they'll think of me when they are in a position to make a referral.

Lastly, we offer our prospects invitations to our events. This allows us to communicate with prospects who may have gone radio silent without resorting to never-ending asks. Instead, we offer them an exclusive, special, and unique event.

Here's the rub in all of this offering: Prospects do not have to attend an event for us to receive a benefit. Simply inviting them tends to put us on a different plane from other M&A advisors. I am currently working leads that I've generated merely from inviting them to events. If we do this enough, I am convinced that some of a firm's "radio silent" leads will self-select and reemerge as viable leads.

Techniques
The techniques I use are tried and true. They are a mix of high tech and high touch. Other than being the author of one of the key components of this plan, I don't claim to have a magic approach. The fact is anyone (with a suitable outgoing, quick witted personality) could do most of this. Instead, the key is consistency — the plan won't work unless it is consistently executed.

The components are as follows:

1. Email blasts
2. Meetings with referral sources (wealth managers, lawyers, accountants, commercial bankers)
3. Meetings with private equity firms
4. Meetings with prospects
5. Business owner events (in conjunction with wealth management, lawyer, accountant)
6. Commercial banker events
7. Website
8. Social media
9. Speaking
10. Providing professional referrals
11. Original articles
12. Informal events (happy hours)

13. Traditional events (sporting events, golf, concerts, theater, etc)
14. Miscellaneous

Email Blasts

Email blasts are designed to keep the firm name in front of people and will be sent to prospects, former clients, referral sources, and friends of the firm. Beyond conveying interesting content, regular emails help with basic branding and name recognition. Even if people don't read the emails, they tend to remember the logo/firm name.

The content of the emails can range from deal announcements, original content, M&A industry stats and news, general business and economic news, statistics and news for specific verticals, marketing/biz dev ideas, leadership ideas, humor, word play, and more. I've found mixing an authoritative and expert voice with some pop culture references, humor, and irreverence goes a long way toward creating memorable and actionable content.

Being the author of a book also means I have a readymade supply of content. I've been excerpting parts of the book (I call it "Lessons from M&A For Dummies"). This provides a large supply of content and works as a form of third party validation.

A program such as Constant Contact (or the like) should be used to easily conform to Can-Spam laws as well as to track click throughs. Adding hyperlinks is a great way to learn who is clicking on what. For example, clicking on the links to the firm's service offerings might warrant a follow up.

Frequency: Email blasts will be sent twice a month, on Tuesdays.

Meetings with Referral Sources and PE Firms
Meetings with referral sources and PE firms will be done twice a week (Tuesday and Thursday) at regular times: 7:30 a.m. (breakfast), 9:00 a.m., 10:30 a.m., noon (lunch), 2:00 p.m., 3:30 p.m.

Prior to each meeting, I study the appointment — the person's background and firm history — and if at all possible, find something I can offer (participation in an event, an introduction, assistance, etc). Anyone I meet with will be added to our email distribution list.

The goal of these meetings is to create prospect leads, opportunities, and partners for our business owner events. Staying in front of people in face-to-face meetings helps keeps the firm's name top of mind.

Frequency: Twice a week (Tuesday and Thursday), twelve meetings per week.

Meetings with Prospects
The goal of all of this marketing is to meet with prospects. I am targeting Mondays, Wednesdays, and Fridays for meetings with prospects.

Frequency: TBD

Business Owner Events
Business owner events are designed for ten to fifteen attendees (business owners or executives only). This intimate setting helps avoid the "cattle call" experience of other groups who pack in two hundred or three hundred attendees and then push them to sign up for a service at the event.

I deliver a presentation that references material from my book. We give a copy of the book and the presentation to all attendees. The presentation contains page numbers which allow the attendees to essentially use *M&A For Dummies* as a text book.

My presentations include:
> M&A related ("How to Enhance Valuation in a Business Sale" and "Why Understanding the M&A Process Can Improve Results")
> Networking and marketing ("Networked to Death")
> Business owner succession ("The Kids Are Not Alright")
> Acquisition ("The Approach")

Since we invite our referral sources to participate, we benefit from offering them something. We also benefit from getting a chance to meet with their invitees. Participants help defray the cost of the event, which are relatively small (approximately $600 for materials plus the cost of the room and food). Please see the "Business Owner Events" document for more detail.

Frequency: Once a month

Commercial Banker Events
As described above, I am offering commercial bankers the chance to set up an event where I'll deliver my "Networked to Death" presentation to their prospects and clients. We also may want to invite our prospects to the event.

Frequency: four times a year.

Website

The website should make it easy for referral sources and prospects to work with us. The website should have a "join our mailing list" button as well as clear-cut calls to action (contact certain people to set up meetings, to ask for referrals, etc.)

The overriding theme of the website should be communication with our target markets (referral sources and prospects).

Digital (Social Media)

Business owners are not going to stay in touch with us via LinkedIn, Facebook, et al. Instead, a digital strategy is meant to keep in touch with our referral sources and friends of the firm, demonstrate our expertise in this new medium, and expand the reach of the firm. The firm should maintain a presence on Twitter, Facebook, Google+, and LinkedIn.

In terms of connecting with prospects, I recommend creating videos for YouTube and lessons for Udemy.

Every employee's signature should contain links to the firm's social media sites as well as a "join our mailing list" link.

Frequency: Four tweets per day — two industry related, one general business/economy related, one personal/fun/irreverent tweet (golf, movies, a joke, sports, music, etc.) Tweets will be forwarded to LinkedIn, Facebook, and Google+. One new YouTube video per month. I have a twelve-part lesson plan (using *M&A For Dummies*) designed for Udemy (I haven't shot it yet).

Speaking

I take advantage of every speaking engagement that is offered to me. In the past year I've lectured at Kellogg and DePaul, I've participated as a panelist at Harvard Business School, I've delivered a presentation to the University Club's professional networking group, and I've been a speaker at a Dan Kennedy "boot camp" event for entrepreneurs.

I accept every offer to speak so I can continue to practice my public speaking. Speaking also helps with brand building and becomes fodder for the firm's newsletter. All firm professionals should be encouraged to seek out (and accept) as many speaking engagements as possible.

Providing Professional Referrals

Providing professional referrals is an age-old technique. But instead of merely providing a short list of names, we should also offer to handle the difficult task of notifying the firms the recipient did not pick. Taking care of the uncomfortable task of closing the loop not only takes away a burden from the recipient, but also gives us another touch point with a professional referral source.

This service/approach should be listed on the website. It is simply something else we can offer referral sources and prospects.

Original Article
An article, written by me or someone else at the firm, will be placed in an email blast and archived on the firm's website. We also can offer the content to other periodicals.

Frequency: Once a month, 600-800 words.

Informal events
Informal "happy hour" mixers at a downtown watering hole are a great way to connect (or reconnect) with leads, former clients, and referral sources in an environment that is more relaxed than official meetings. I use a cash bar, thus these events have little to no cost to the firm.

Frequency: Once a month, Wednesday or Thursday, 5 to 9 p.m. River North locations work very well.

Traditional Events
Tried and true events such as golf outings and tickets to sporting events and shows can be part of the marketing mix.

Miscellaneous
Additional branding can be generated from ad specialties (golf balls, coffee mugs with the firm's logo and tag line). As far as tag lines, what a company does should be able to be conveyed on a golf ball.

Pitches
I will attend meeting with prospects. Ideally, I will be joined by another senior member of the firm. One of the "leave behinds" we can use is a copy of *M&A For Dummies*. I recommend affixing a business card or sticker with the firm's name and contact info.

Alternatively, we can give prospects a tablet with *M&A Dummies*, other firm resources, plus any other relevant industry data and articles. We can include a FedEx envelope and tell them if they become our client, the tablet is theirs to keep. If they decide to not work with us, we simply ask them to return the tablet. This forces the prospect to act affirmatively: either they hire us or they signal they don't want to do anything (or work with us) by returning the tablet.

The Hand Off

After a client is signed, and depending upon the needs of the firm and the client, I can either remain involved in the process or we can do a clean "hand off" to the execution team.

My Role

Nominally, my role is business development, but we should not use that term in my title. I do not want business development or origination in my bio. In my opinion, no one's bio should mention origination. Anyone who interacts with us will be interacting with a senior person/deal maker and not business development or sales person.

Malleability and References

This plan is adjustable. Please do not construe anything as static. Instead, this plan is designed to form the basis of further discussions and refinement.

The Emails

I stay in touch with certain professional by writing periodic emails. Here's a sample of some of them.

Wed 4/23/2014 8:58 A.M.
Subject: Please excuse the mass email, but this is urgent. Extremely urgent.

We have 4 Cubs tickets for the game tomorrow afternoon. Game time is 1:20 p.m. That's Thursday April 24 in case you're reading this email a day late. And 2014, in case this email got stuck in your spam filter and you're reading this email in some future year. If that's the case, do we have flying cars yet?

Anyway, back to the tickets. Yeah. I know. The Cubs. April. Chicago. But the forecast says a high of 62 degrees, that's Fahrenheit for you Luddite fans of old-style measurements or 16.67 degrees Celsius for you hipster metric types. So the weather should be pretty good and just in case the game is interrupted by rain, the seats are protected by the grandstand. You'll stay dry while the suckers with "better" tickets get soaked.

The other challenge we face is my entire office is at a limited partners powwow. This means I am alone today and I have no administrative help. My first thought was to have a kegger. But I decided against that because keggers get messy and I'd have to clean up. So instead, I've decided to give away baseball tickets. Since I don't have anyone to arrange safe passage of the tickets — I'll have to hand deliver them to you. Alternatively, if you have a young charge in your employ seeking to earn brownie points, you can send your lackey to pick them up.

If you're interested, let me know.

Bill

Tue 4/29/2014 12:34 P.M.
Subject: Cubs tickets for 5/3 and an explanation

Sometimes you make an investment. That investment might be something personal — setting up a college fund for the kids or planning for your retirement. Sometimes you make a business investment — new computers or manufacturing equipment or personnel. Or sometimes you invest in something truly important, you know, a new set of golf clubs that will help you break 80. "This is it," you tell yourself, "this is the final piece that will help me break 80! It's not the Indian, it's the arrows! It's gonna happen this time! All I needed to turn around my faltering golf game was to pair new equipment with my same, crumby golf swing!"

And sometimes you bump your head, fall down a flight of stairs, get hit by a cab, and get struck by lightning while on your way to a marketing meeting and in your fried, concussed stupor you have an epiphany: "Hey! Let's invest in marketing by buying season tickets for the Cubs!"

That's what we did and that's why I'm emailing you. So the good news is you're in my trusted circle. This means you'll be getting emails like this from me on a regular basis. The bad news is you're in my trusted circle and that means you'll be getting emails like this from me on a regular basis.

We have 4 tickets to the game on Saturday. May 3, 12:05 start. Cubs vs. the hated Cardinals. If you'd like all or some of the tickets, let me know.

If you don't want to receive any more emails like this, just let me know and I'll take you off my list. If you think any of your colleagues would like to receive my wondrous emails bearing gifts of corporate largess, feel free to forward this to them. If they contact me, I'll add them to my list.

Bill

Mon 6/2/2014 6:29 P.M.
Subject: Cubs tickets available for Wednesday June 4

Yes, yes, I know. Many of you seem to think the Cubs are having a bad season. That might be true if you're one of those sticklers who views baseball success and failure through the narrow, beady little eyes of win-loss records. But since the Cubs will be playing the Mets of New York City, perhaps we should examine baseball in a slightly different way.

Recently, the nabobs at the New York Times created a nifty interactive map showing baseball fan allegiance by zip code. Please follow this link:

http://www.nytimes.com/interactive/2014/04/24/upshot/facebook-baseball-map.html#5,38.669,-94.799

If you spend a lot of time goofing around with this map instead of, you know, working, you'll be hard pressed to find any zip code where the Mets have a plurality of fans. Go on. I triple dog dare you! As you'll soon discover, Cubs Nation — despite the inexplicable grayish-black stain in the middle of it — is far larger than Mets Nation, which, as far as I can tell, doesn't exist.

So never fear, gentle email pal, regardless of the outcome on the field on June 4, the Cubs are the true victors! Well, if Internet generated maps were the only measuring stick.

More importantly, if you'd like tickets to the game on June 4, I have four available. First to respond gets them. 7:05 p.m. start time.

Bill

Mon 6/23/2014 6:24 P.M.
Subject: Cubs tickets available for Thursday, June 26

In case you've been too busy to notice, the sun recently passed its highest point in the sky. The optimist says this marks the beginning of summer. The pessimist realizes we have just begun the long, slow descent into winter. And whether you are an optimist or pessimist, one thing is true: you are receiving this email because I have four tickets to the game on Thursday.

The optimist will be happy at the prospect of getting free Cubs tickets. The pessimist will complain about the 7:05 p.m. start time because that means playing hooky from work by going to a baseball game "for business reasons" is out of the equation. Sorry, you will have to put in a full day of toil.

The Cubs are playing the Canadian Expats, also known as the Washington Nationals. Ironically, the Canadian Expats have no Canadian players, which, as I think about it, is probably the reason they fled Montreal. And they've been pretty good in recent years, so this is your change to take a gander, up close and personal, at what a team with a winning records looks like.

If you'd like all or some of the tickets, let me know. First to respond gets 'em!

Bill

Tue 6/24/2014 6:36 P.M.
Subject: Happy hour – Thursday 6/26 at Randolph Tavern

I know, I know, I have you trained like Pavlov's dog to expect every email from me to contain an offer of Cubs tickets. Well, sorry to disappoint; this missive contains nary an offer of sporting tickets.

Instead, I am inviting you to join a group of Chicago's top professionals for a once in a life time happy hour. That's right! This is the only time this event will be held on June 26, 2014. We will never again hold this event on June 26, 2014. Ever again! Never. This is it.

We're gathering at the newly opened Randolph Tavern, a swank, cavernous, and curiously named tavern located at 188 W. Randolph. I wonder where they got the name. Anyway, just say you're with the "Bill Snow group" and assuming you're not asked to leave, someone will point you to the section where we have gathered.

Activities will include: standing, sitting, drinking adult beverages, talking, handing out business cards, standing, shifting uncomfortably on your feet as you rethink your decision to give up your seat to someone else, more drinking, and eventually, going home.

No need to RSVP, just show up. Feel free to bring friends, if you have any, and if you are sans friends, feel free to bring coworkers, well, those who still talk to you.

The fun starts at 5 p.m. and ends when you go home. I hope to see you Thursday after work.

Bill

Mon 7/28/2014 3:48 P.M.
Subject: Cubs ticket available for July 31

Have you ever woken in the morning, especially during the summer, and thought, "What am I doing to myself? A career, work, mortgage, responsibilities...how the heck did that happen? When did I grow up? I don't want to go to work today. I want to go to

Wrigley Field and watch the last place Cubs play some other last place team!"

Well, now's your chance to play hooky from grown up responsibilities; I have a ticket for you.

That's right, I have a single, solitary ticket for the Cubs game on Thursday July 31, 1:20 p.m. start. And if that's not exciting enough, I'll be attending the game, too. As far as the Cubs' opponent....let's see, uh, er, well, who cares?!?!

 First to respond gets the ticket. Hope to see you on Thursday!

Bill

Fri 8/15/2014 4:44 P.M.
Subject: At my signal, unleash Cubs tix for Aug 23rd

Greetings professionals, semi-professionals, and all manner of creatures who might be reading this missive; I extend to you this laurel...and hardy email. See, I'm adding a little something to this email. As you all know first prize is a Cadillac. Second prize is a set of steak knives. Third prize is you get Cubs tickets. Get the picture? You laughing now?

Full disclosure, I don't have the Cadillac or the steak knives, but I do have the Cubs tickets!

That's right! I have four tickets available for the game on August 23rd. That's a Saturday and the game is a 1:20 p.m. start. Normally I'd snatch up these tickets for myself but since I have a nasty addiction — I play this thing called "golf," maybe you've heard of it — I am unable to go to the game.

Instead, I'll be sitting in my car on the way home from the golf course, hoping the texting-while-driving knucklehead behind me doesn't rear-end my car. By the way, if you are wont to text and drive, I have one thing to say to you: leave the cannoli; take the Cubs tickets.

"The Cubs," you're thinking to yourself, "I'm shocked, SHOCKED, to learn you're giving away Cubs tickets." Well, let me retort. When you're dying in your bed, many years from now, would you be willing to trade ALL the days, from this day to that, for one chance, just one chance, to come back here and take those darn Cubs tickets?

Of course you would. I want you to remember that no knucklehead ever won Cubs tickets by texting and driving. He won them by making the other poor dumb knucklehead text for his country. So fill your hand, you son of a Sandberg, and pretty please, with sugar on top, someone take these tickets!

First to respond gets the tickets. First to correctly identify all of the movies referenced in my homage wins a cocktail of your choice at the Loop drinking establishment of your choice. The downside is you'll have to have the drink with me.

Have a great weekend!

Bill

Fri 8/29/2014 6:04 P.M.
Subject: Here Comes a Regular…offer of Cubs tickets

As you're about to leave the office for the holiday weekend — and I'm sure you're working past 5 p.m. today, no knocking off early for you, right? — I have yet another offer of Cubs tickets.

"Cubs tickets," you're now muttering to yourself, "of course his email is about Cubs tickets. Why else would he send me an email as the day passes quittin' time o'clock? Cubs tickets. Sheesh!"

You're right. I'm not just sending you an email with an offer of Cubs tickets. If you've received these emails before you know that I can't make the giveaway of tickets an easy thing. So instead, I'm using this missive to send you a link to the great Fenway organist Josh Kantor rocking the house with his baseball organ version of a new Bob Mould tune. Fans of good music, please follow this link. https://www.youtube.com/watch?v=AV_7cyjmyEg

Also, I have been remiss this summer. I have not been diligent in putting my golf list together. So, much like the Cubs, this list will have to be for next year. If you golf and would like to be on my golf list, send me an email. We'll try to "tee it up." Maybe, if we get crazy, we can try to bring a prospect or two to join us. If you want to be on my golf list, click this.

Now that we have all that other stuff out of the way, on to the real reason for the email…Cubs tickets! I have four tickets to the game on Friday September 5, 1:20 p.m. start. This means if you go to the game, you get to play hooky from work. Further, that means your work week will be only three days. Lucky you.

If you would like some or all of the tickets, let me hear ya! A one, a two, a three...first to respond gets 'em.

Bill

As you may have noticed, fall has pounced upon Chicago. Summer is over, and uh, you might say winter is coming. But a bit more baseball remains and the Cubs, so hear me roar, are definitely in the ascent. Ours is the fury! Well, except for the past few games, granted, but since and the Cubs are growing stronger, I have no doubt better days are ahead. These young Cubbies are going to prove they are unbowed, unbent, unbroken. Someday their play will be as high as honor.

Before we get back to baseball talk, I need to mention I'm hosting a very casual networking shindig at Tradition (160 N Franklin) next week. That's Thursday September 18, 5 to 8 p.m. You can peruse the registration here. Or just show up. And if you show up and tell me the theme of this email I'll buy you a drink. Not mead and meat! Just a humble little drink.

And now, on to the giveaway portion of today's email. I have four tickets available for the game on Monday September 15. The game is a 7:05 start, so you will have to put in a full day of work before heading to the park. If you're interested in all or some of the tickets, contact me. First to respond gets 'em!

And if you can't make the game or my networking shindig but you'd like to get together, let me know. We'll get something on the calendar. We have so much to talk about... a surfeit of capital, massive amounts of liquidity, and amazing valuations. But is that window shutting? Is winter coming for these valuations? Reach out to me if you're interested in talking further.

We do not sow!

Bill

The equinox. There. I said it. The equinox is upon us and as far as I'm concerned, you only have two options. Option one is to spend Monday Sept 22 standing on an east-west street staring at the sun as it rises directly due east and then staring at the sun again when it sets 12 hours later directly due west. If you're an equinox geek like me you enjoy watching the sun rise and set RIGHT DOWN THE MIDDLE OF THE STREET! Holy cow, that's really cool!

For those of you who think the equinox always occurs on the 21st, let me be the one to ruin a few things for you...the Easter Bunny, Santa Claus, the Tooth Fairy, suburbanites who can parallel park, and a well called game by Joe Buck, these are all fictions and do not exist.

And you can add to your newly minted fiction list the fallacy of the equinox always falling on the 21st. The 2014 autumnal equinox occurs at 9:29 p.m. Central Daylight Time on Sept 22. OK, got it? Not on the 21st. The 22nd. Don't believe me? Here, read this. It's on the Internet so it must be true.
http://www.timeanddate.com/calendar/september-equinox.html

However, if you are dead set in your ways and want to believe the Equinox is on the 21st, then option two is to celebrate your fake equinox by taking in a ball game at the old ballpark. That's right, gentle reader, I have four tickets available for the game on Sunday the 21st. 1:20 p.m. start.

First to respond get's 'em!

Bill

Mon 9/22/2014 2:38 P.M.
Subject: The end is nigh (well, for the 2014 baseball season)

The 2014 Cubs season is starting to wind down. I like to think that that season began its "wind down" sometime in April, but you know what? I'm not going to make that cheap joke! Let the other M&A advisors who send you snappy emails with offers of free things take that low road. My missives take the high road.
https://www.youtube.com/watch?v=c-jKfLXYQqw

Speaking of the low road, the hated St. Louis Cardinals are in Chicago for a series against the Cubs. For those of you unfamiliar with Chicago history, let me give you a little bit of the backstory. When polluted water from the Chicago River surged miles into Lake Michigan, overflowing the intake cribs and contaminating the city's drinking water system, engineers reversed the flow of the Chicago River and pumped the city's sewage to the Illinois River and ultimately the Mississippi River and St. Louis. To this day, more than a century later, Cardinal fans still harbor ill will toward their aquatically superior neighbors to the north. This is the crux of the Cubs-Cardinals rivalry.

Now you know the rest of the story.

And yes, I have tickets four available for the game on Wednesday, September 24. The game is a 7:05 p.m. start. These are the last set of Cubs tickets I have to give away for this season. First to respond [long Paul Harvey pause] gets 'em!

Good day!

Bill

The Invitation

I host occasional casual networking events. Since I am unable to write normal invitations, they end up looking like this.

Drinks At Tradition

Bill Snow

Thursday, September 18, 2014 from 5:00 P.M. to 8:00 P.M. (CDT)
Chicago, IL

Event Details
Join some of Chicago's top professionals as we gather for a few adult-style beverages at Tradition (160 N Franklin). No agenda, no speakers — no plan, come to think of it — just a casual time with some good people. Bill will be the master of ceremonies, so don't worry if you don't know anyone; you will after the event is done. Just ask for Bill and the staff will point you in the right direction.

The event does have strict requirements for attendees. You need to be able to sit, stand, talk, and perhaps partake in a beverage.

This event is open to anyone who wants to show up. Just bring some business cards...you never know when you'll make a connection.

TICKETS (pick one)

Super Special Deluxe Early Bird (Free Admittance)
This ticket is designed for early birds. You like to show off to other people that you sign up for things before all others. Other than that, this admittance is no different than any other. Not good for free drinks.

Regular (Free Admittance)
You're just an average Joe, and frankly, you're OK with that. You don't need to proclaim yourself some sort of networking guru. You're sturdy, steady, dependable, professional, sometimes you come up with interesting asides, jokes, puns, and quips. And once in awhile, when you've had too much coffee, you come up with truly transcendent philosophical anecdotes and observations. As far as a regular Joe, you're one of a kind! Not

good for free drinks.

Last Minute (Free Admittance)

You wait until the last minute to do everything, and you know what, you don't give a rat's bar stool about it. People will wait. They'll be there when you show up. Why the heck should you, a true last minute pro, be bothered with the prosaic concerns of time-obsessed neurotics? You're OK. We're all OK. You'll be there. Eventually. Not good for free drinks.

Networking Novice (Free Admittance)

Don't be afraid, little one, no one will bite you. The sound will be turned down and no one will make quick moves. After all, your skittish nature might knock over someone's beer, so we will tread with care and make sure you have a good time. Not good for free drinks.

Wise Old Sage (Free Admittance)

And here's to you, wise old sage, our nation turns its networking eyes to you. See us, hear us, feel us, lead us. O great sage, show us the way to networking nirvana and glory. Not good for free drinks.

Know-It-All (Free Admittance)

Yeah, yeah, yeah, you've done it all a million times and you know it all. And everyone knows this because you, the god guru of networking, tell everyone that you know everything. So despite your world weary outlook, you have deigned this event, and by proxy, the other attendees, worthy of your haughty presence. For those about to network, we salute you. Not good for free drinks.

One Of A Kind (Free Admittance)

This is it. The only one. And you grabbed it. No one else will get this ticket. You're special. You win life. Granted, this ticket won't get you anything unavailable to others...but who cares...YOU GOT THE ONLY ONE! Not good for free drinks.

None Of The Above (Free Admittance)

If you've ever felt the need to drive someplace, just to be surly, if none of the other tickets provided the right existential perspective for our baseborn mortal coil, then you've found your home amongst the great nation of none of the above. Not good for free drinks.

FAQs

Do I need an ID to enter the event?

You need to be 21 or older to drink adult-style beverages in the United States. This isn't Amsterdam, pal! So, despite the gray in what's left of your hair, you might need to show ID.

What are my transport/parking options getting to the event?

You gotta figure out some things on your own. I can't do everything for you. Have you heard of Google maps?

Are drinks and food being provided at no cost to me?

Sorry, pal, you gotta pay your own freight. This is a CASUAL event. In case you're not good at picking up hints and reading between the lines, the word casual is a euphemism for, "you're on your own, pal, we ain't paying for you."

Seriously? You're not paying for my drinks and food? What a rip off!

You're really having a tough time with this, aren't you? You have to pay for your own drinks and food!

Should I tip the wait staff?

I am shocked, SHOCKED to learn that you would ask such a thing. Of course you need to tip the person who brings you drinks. Shesh!

What can/can't I bring to the event?

Bring business cards; leave the cannoli.

Where can I contact the organizer with any questions?

You can send Bill an email, if you dare: bill@billsnow.com

Is my registration/ticket transferrable?

If you can find some other sucker who will take your ticket, go for it!

Can I update my registration information?

I really don't care what you do in your private life, so yeah, pretty please, with sugar on it, update your darn registration information. Just leave me out of your reindeer games.

Do I have to bring my printed ticket to the event?

Of course not! If you haven't figured it out by now, the tickets are a goof! A bit of fluff, some fun. But the event is real and we hope to see you.

What is the refund policy?

You've got some nerve, pal. This event is free to enter and you're already asking for a refund? Unbelievable!

The name on the registration/ticket doesn't match the attendee. Is that okay?

This is ok so long as the ticket holder is willing to go through event remediation. Step one is to admit you have a problem, step two is to shrug your shoulders and enter the event, step three is to order a drink, and step four is to talk to someone.

What are you still doing here?
Hey, pal! The book is done. If you liked it feel free to connect to Bill. Heck, if you didn't like it, you can connect with him anyway.

Facebook: https://www.facebook.com/BillSnowFanPage
LinkedIn: http://www.linkedin.com/in/billsnow
Twitter: http://www.twitter.com/bill_snow

Check out Bill's website, www.billsnow.com or send him an email, if you dare, bill@billsnow.com

And if you're feeling particularly adventurous, give him a review on Amazon: http://www.amazon.com/author/billsnow

Other books by Bill Snow

Mergers & Acquisitions For Dummies

Venture Capital 101

www.ingramcontent.com/pod-product-compliance
Lightning Source LLC
Chambersburg PA
CBHW070806180526
45168CB00002B/509